Dec '84

A
Limited
First Printing

Jerry Gildemeister

Don Gray

People would ask—

"Why in the world did your folks ever come to this Godforsaken place when they could have had a much easier life in the Grande Ronde Valley?"

If only I could make them see with our eyes the way it looked to us, coming from Missouri—all clean, lovely waving grass, cold water, tall trees, and mountain scenery too beautiful for words to describe.

Daisy Wasson

A Limited First Printing · 1989

The Bear Wallow Publishing Company
Union, Oregon

Around the Cat's Back

by *Jerry Gildemeister*
as compiled from the writing and diaries of Daisy and Caroline Wasson
with Photography and Design by Gildemeister
and Watercolor Illustrations by **Don Gray**

═══ Credits ═══

Writing (as compiled from the manuscript of Daisy Wasson and
the diary of Caroline Wasson), photography, and book design—
by Jerry Gildemeister.

Watercolor artwork—by Don Gray.

Typography set in Weiss and Janson—by Gildemeister.

Photographic production—by Cathy Gildemeister.

Color separations—by Cascade Color of Portland, Oregon.

Text paper—Mead Signature Dull supplied by
Fraser Paper Company of Portland, Oregon.

End Papers—Astroparche Cover supplied by
Idaho Pacific Paper of Boise, Idaho.

Printing—by The Irwin-Hodson Company of Portland, Oregon.

Bindery—by Lincoln & Allen Company of Portland, Oregon.

Library of Congress Cataloging-in-Publication Data

Gildemeister, Jerry, 1934—

Summary:
A compilation of writing by Daisy Wasson and diary by
Caroline Wasson of their childhood experiences on a
Wallowa Mountain homestead in northeast Oregon from
1886 through 1896. Illustrated with family photographs,
original watercolors by Don Gray, and photographic
images by Gildemeister.

Around the Cat's Back
by Jerry Gildemeister: with watercolor illustrations by Don Gray,
and photography by Gildemeister: compiled from the writing of
Daisy Wasson and the diary of Caroline Wasson.
p. cm.

1. Wallowa River Valley (Or.)—Social life and customs.
2. Frontier and pioneer life—Oregon—Wallowa River Valley.
3. Wasson, Daisy—Childhood and youth.
4. Wasson, Caroline—Childhood and youth.
I. Gray, Don, 1948— . II. Title.

F882.W2G55 1989   979.5'73—dc20   89-17945 CIP

ISBN 0-936376-06-6 . . . . $32.50.

6

About the Book

In 1987 Grace Bartlett, curator of the Wallowa County Museum in Joseph, Oregon, sent us a manuscript written by Daisy Wasson who, along with her sister Caroline, grew up on a homestead near Oregon's majestic Wallowa Mountains. As we delved into the background of the story, we discovered that Caroline kept a diary while on the homestead, and the sisters later corresponded about their childhood experiences. The more we researched the more enthused we became with the notion of creating a book with the material at hand. Here were two young girls whose parents brought them to the wilds of northeast Oregon in 1885 to homestead. Although the family was isolated from civilization, and they endured long harsh winters and many other hardships, they loved this home site, living a very simple, but wonderful, ten years on the Divide, a long open ridge running north from the Wallowa Mountains and separating Big Sheep from Little Sheep Creek.

When we visited the area we could see why this place was so special to them—there, high on the open ridge, is a setting that can only be described as *Awesome!* From their cabin site the family had an uninterupted view of Idaho's Seven Devils mountains to the east, and Oregon's magnificent Wallowas to the southwest. To the north, across Coyote Creek canyon, the Cat's Back Ridge seems to go on forever. Interspersed in all directions are timbered draws that fall into deep canyons leading toward the mighty Snake River canyon.

The uniqueness of homesteading from a child's point of view and the magnificient setting compelled us to create *Around the Cat's Back*, a wonderful journey back in time to join Daisy and Caroline Wasson experiencing their childhood in the wilds of Oregon's Wallowa Mountains.

We are deeply indebted to Grace Bartlett who brought Daisy's writing and Caroline's diary to our attention, and to Corneil Hughes, Caroline's daughter, who so graciously consented to their use for this book project. Also, we wish to thank the Wallowa and Union county museums for their cooperation in securing artifacts for use in the book illustration.

We invite you now to journey back in time to join the Wasson family and their homesteading adventures in *Around the Cat's Back*.

Cathy Gildemeister
The Bear Wallow Publishing Company

The Wasson Family
Joseph, Jennie, Daisy & Caroline

Introduction

As the West was opened to settlement in the 1840s thousands of wagon train families followed the Oregon Trail westward in search of a new life in the untamed wilderness. With the opening of the transcontinental railroad in 1869 and the completion of the branch line to the Pacific Northwest in 1884, many families who could muster the rate of passage chose these safer and much faster routes to a new home.

One of these families who traveled by emigrant train to the Northwest was the Wasson family. Their reason for seeking a new life in the West differed from most families, for Caroline had contracted spinal meningitis, and her doctor recommended the drier climate of the West, for he believed it would be better for her health.

So, in 1885, the Wassons left their home in Nevada, Missouri and headed for the Wallowa Valley of northeast Oregon where relatives and other families from Missouri had previously settled. The area had been opened to homesteading in 1871 and the choice land in the valleys had been taken up by the time the Wassons arrived, so Joseph decided on a plot of ground situated on an open ridge called *the Divide*.

The homestead site was a long eighteen miles to any semblance of civilization, and their closest neighbor was over two miles away, but the family loved this place on the high open bench with its awesome view of the surrounding mountains. One Christmas Caroline received her first diary, and began an account of daily life, recording common events as well as cherished memories and troubled times. The sisters corresponded over the years, recalling their childhood experiences, and nearly fifty years after leaving the homestead, Daisy sat down to write of their family life on the Divide.....

Daisy Wasson . . . . .

In our log-cabin pioneer home the *Wheeler and Wilson* sewing machine stood first in importance.

Since we were snowed in for nearly six months every year, Mama kept busy sewing all of our clothes. This machine was her prized possession, and she used to boast proudly that the cabinet was of solid walnut. It got only the best of care — no carpet-rag sewing, no quilt piecing, or mending was allowed, because starting and stopping it so often would wear it out faster. It was never loaned out, nor was anyone permitted to sew on it who was not careful to start and stop it slowly.

Caroline and I loved the cabinet drawers. They were so smooth and nicely made. When I was six and Caroline was four, Mama, much to our joy, gave each of us one of the drawers for our very own. Caroline, because she was so little, had the lowest one, the next one was mine, and the top one was Mama's. We kept our sewing things and other treasures in these drawers. I recall that Caroline had a spool of blue cotton thread and I a pink one.

In Mama's drawer, among her thread and other things, was an object that to my childish mind was a thing of great beauty, and for which I longed with all my heart. It was a small piece of red sealing wax. Many times Mama was asked to tell how she came by it, and we never grew tired of hearing the story. When she was a very small girl in Missouri her father bought a new grindstone, and his neighbors often came to use it, to sharpen their axes and other farm tools. One day a man came with a new axe. Mama was asked to turn the grindstone for the man, and he promised to give her something pretty for her work. So, when his axe was sharp he presented the reward—a small piece of red sealing wax. It was one of her few childhood treasures, and was always kept in the top drawer of the sewing machine. We could take it out and look at it, but we must always be careful to return it to the top drawer.

Caroline and I, in due time, grew up and were married. Papa passed away, and for many years Mama lived alone. When she was no longer able to live by herself, I traveled to Vancouver, Washington, from my home in Michigan, to take her back with me for the rest of her days. It is hard to break up an old home and part with life-time treasures, but Mama never shed a tear. We went through chests and closets, choosing what things she wanted to keep. She sat, and I carried things to her to examine. When we went through the old sewing machine, she looked at the lower drawer first, and, as she handed it back to me she murmured, "The bottom drawer was Caroline's, the middle one was Daisy's, the top one was mine."

While going through the contents of the top one she suddenly looked up at me and held up the piece of red sealing wax.

"Wouldn't you like to have this?" she asked.

Would I? Indeed! I realized that I had always wanted it, all my life, and after more than sixty years it was at last to be mine.

Seeing that little piece of red wax suddenly took my thoughts back to our wonderful childhood on the homestead in the Wallowa Country of Northeast Oregon. . . . .

Heading West

In the spring of 1885, when I was four years old, my family headed West from Missouri to Oregon on an emigrant train. There was my Grandmother Blevans, Uncle Steve, who was eighteen, nine-year-old Aunt Allie, my parents, Jennie and Joseph, two-year-old sister Caroline, and myself, Daisy Wasson.

We took our own feather beds, and food which we cooked on the train. There was boiled ham, homemade bread, jelly, dried fruit, and a wonderful big, round, boiled sausage which my Grandmother Wasson had stuffed in a pig's stomach. I remember screaming loudly on saying good-bye to this grandmother, and saying, "I will never see my grandmother any more!" And I never did.

I didn't know we were on the train. I thought when it started that the buildings we were passing were moving, instead of us.

We reached La Grande, Oregon, the end of the railroad for us, to find that cousin Rat Blevans had not come yet with his team and wagon to take us the remaining seventy-five miles. There was no hotel, and we had no money for one if there had been, so we made our beds on the floor of a house that was being built. There was a stove for cooking, and after several days of waiting, Rat finally came to take us to the Wallowa Valley. I will never forget the long ride we took that last week of April. We rode for miles through the valley and over rolling hills. Along the way there were beautiful wild flowers. I remember thinking that Rat had fallen off the wagon when he had only jumped down to pick some flowers for Caroline and me.

Then there was a tortuous stretch through great canyons, down a winding mountainous grade, the likes of which we had never seen before, and along beautiful, clear-flowing rivers.

We were to stay at Mama's Uncle Jeff Blevans' cabin. It was located in the most beautiful valley surrounded by rolling hills and magnificent mountains. Far to the east was a rugged range called the *Salmon River* or *Seven Devils Mountains*.

Great-uncle Jeff had left Missouri when he was nineteen and come to Oregon. He had married, but not too long afterwards was left a widower with three small boys to raise as best he could. They were well-loved, but did lead a queer hit-and-miss life in the wilds of Oregon. It was most unusual that the boys were allowed to name themselves, and the eldest chose Murat, or *Rat* for short.

Their cabin was a sore disappointment to my parents, as Uncle Jeff and his boys had been living there since 1877, and everything was far from clean. There was one room with a fireplace, benches, and bunks that were built one above the other at the rear of the room.

To one side was a shed-kitchen with a small legless cookstove sitting in a box of dirt.

Papa, with the help of Rat and Steve, built more bunks, and after some vigorous scrubbing we settled in for the coming year. I don't know if we paid rent, but I doubt that we did, for Papa had only $60 when we reached Oregon, and Grandma just a little more.

I was too young to remember much of our stay there, but I do recall that there was a creek running by the cabin and I fell into it one day. There was quite a scrambling of all the grownups, and I quite enjoyed the attention I got — being wrapped up in a quilt and sitting in Grandma's rocker by the fire.

Homesteading the Divide

By the time we got to the Wallowa Valley most of the best land had been taken up since the area was opened to homesteading in 1871. So Papa chose some high level ground along the Divide ridge between Little Sheep Creek and Big Sheep Creek. This was about eighteen miles east of Joseph and just south of the long bare ridge known as the Cat's Back. To the east were the Seven Devils Mountains and to the southwest were the Eagle Mountains, often referred to as *The Wallowas*.

All the time Papa could get was spent building a log house with a rock fireplace.

How new and clean and dear that cabin was! It had an eight-paned window, much to the surprise of the other homesteaders. Inside there were boards nailed over the logs, and then newspapers covered the boards, and after a yearly addition during our ten years of life there it made quite a thick covering. Mama always put the papers right side up and we had lots of fun reading from the walls.

I recall one spring when I was about twelve years old, a young and, to us, wonderful man spent the night with us. He was from *Outside*, and could tell us many things we longed to hear about. He happened to notice a picture of Conan Doyle pasted on the wall, as a "young author who has come to public notice," and our guest gave his opinion that Doyle was going to be heard from. I can see that picture yet. It was on one side of the fireplace, and I used to look up and think, "How could he make up stories?" And after reading his last one, *Maracot Deep*, I still wonder. Then Doyle's smug young face disappeared from sight when the next year's layer of paper was pasted up on the wall.

Our cabin was furnished entirely with homemade furniture except for the Wheeler and Wilson sewing machine, the cookstove, and a zinc-covered trunk which held many mysterious articles. The trunk's lock always looked to me like an ugly face when I saw it at night with the firelight flickering on it.

There were two bedsteads in the back of the room. They had slats, a straw mattress, then a feather bed, and the blankets and quilts. Our family took pride in having good beds, and I have often heard them say of someone who was very shiftless, "Why, they don't make their beds till noon!" We always used bolsters with bolster-shams, as well as pillow-shams.

Papa made a huge cupboard, a table, and three benches. One was a long one that Caroline and I sat on when we ate. Usually it was pushed under the table, and after we acquired a cat family, pulling out the bench was a signal that it was mealtime for them.

We had white muslin curtains, a mantel-and-clock shelf, also another shelf—both covered with scalloped newspapers. And there was a gaily-flowered curtain in front of our beds to shut them off from the rest of the room, and another over the place where we hung our clothes. There were crocheted rag rugs, and after we got our big rocker and little rocker our house was nice to look at. Soon there were six wooden chairs with yellow painted, rawhide seats made by a neighbor, Grandpa Bunnell, who was a carpenter. After a few years, a shed-kitchen and a pantry, called *the little room*, were added to our cabin. It was a mere board shed, shut off from the rest of the cabin, and in winter we had to put on overshoes and coats until it got warmed up a bit.

Papa had planed the floor so Caroline would not get splinters in her hands, for she was not yet walking due to her past illness. This was the main reason we came to Oregon, for she had had spinal meningitis just before she was two years old, and the doctor had said that she would be better off in a climate like that of Northeast Oregon. I remember though after she got here that she cried for cornbread and milk and in fear of the high hills. We had no cow and Mama would walk several miles down to our neighbors, the Huffmans, to get a little milk for her once in a while.

Although this home on the Divide was very isolated and far from civilization, it was dear to us all—a place I shall never stop loving all of my life.

The country was new, and though we had neighbors, none were closer than two and a half miles from our cabin. Some were especially good neighbors, particularly the young Bunnells. Their baby, just a few months old, was very cute. But a terrible thing happened that first winter we were on the Divide. Jim, the father, disappeared—he just went out and never returned. His wife, in search of help, waded through the snow to our cabin with their little baby in her arms. Papa went to Jim's father's place and they organized a party to search for him. After several days they found his body where he had slid down a smooth snow-covered hillside on our land, right down over our huckleberry patch.

Uncle Steve wasn't yet old enough to file claim on a piece of land, so he bought Mrs. Bunnell's improvements, but waited until spring before moving into the cabin. We were very glad to have him near us, but we were sorry to lose the Bunnells.

There was another neighbor, a widow with four children nearly grown. We didn't admire her, for she chewed tobacco. Papa also chewed, but that was all right for he was a man. Mrs. Stockley would come to our house, and she and Papa would sit before the fire and have a contest, to see who could spit the farthest and hit a knot-hole in the fire. She always won. One summer when the huckleberries were thick she came to see us and learned that we had a small huckleberry patch on our place. A few days later Mama saw three hats showing just above the brink of the canyon. She knew it was Mrs. Stockley and her daughters. They had sneaked around our place and along the canyon, thinking we could not see them. But their big old black straw hats gave them away. They were after our berries. Mama said, "Let them have them if they can pick them." The berries were very difficult to pick as Mama had to sit at the top of the patch and slide down, then hold onto the short bushes while picking, pull herself back up, empty the bucket, and repeat the process again. Grandma had no use for Mrs. Stockley and said, "Trifling old heifer—why didn't she ask if she could pick some berries?"

Another of our neighbors, the Browns, came from Tennesse to Wallowa Country about 1890. They came by horse-drawn wagon—father, mother, and three children—the oldest a pretty dark-eyed girl of seventeen named Stella, a son of fourteen named Ernest, and a really lovely little girl of about eight named Esther. They were all nice people.

Not long after they had arrived Stella came to our house horseback to get Mama to cut and fit her wedding dress. Mama was pleased to do it, and Caroline and I were thrilled to watch the proceedings.

Some of our other neighbors were the John Fine family who lived along Coyote Creek, the Huffmans, whose place was on Big Sheep Creek; the Needham, Shaw, and Hepburn families, as well as Grandpa Bunnell.

Another of our neighbors, the Pipers, also from Missouri, consisted of Mr. and Mrs. Piper, Sally, Lucy, Joe, and John. The mother called the children by many endearments, such as *lovey* and *kissy*. She wore the sleeves of her dresses so long that she could, and did, use them as pot-holders while cooking.

One day Mama bundled Caroline and me up good and warm and let us ride with Papa in the wagon to get a load of wood from the timber. He went right past the Piper place so we could have the great pleasure of visiting them. Mrs. Piper had baked a batch of cookies and turned them out on a long bench where we could help ourselves while they were still hot. I can still remember how good they were and how lovely she was to us.

When Papa returned with his high load of wood he was surprised to see us with a sack containing a howling cat. Mrs. Piper had given it to us, and I think it must have been the first time in my life that I thanked anyone for a gift unprompted. I felt so proud and grown-up. And I still remember the amused look on Mrs. Piper's face. After we got home, and our mother said what she did, I gathered that we had been worked, for who in world wanted a little calico female cat, with her ears cut straight across?

Our Pet Family

To us our pets were like real people. Some of the most important events that I can remember were when they became a part of our family.

Dear little Croppie was the start of our cat family. Papa had named her *Croppie* because of her cropped ears. Although she was a thief, she was very considerate and gave us only one family a year, but, even so, at one time we had fifteen cats.

The first year we were on the ranch a young yellow tomcat came to us. He *talked* in little short expressive mews, and never did meow like other cats. Tom was never the father of any of our Croppie's kittens for he was a *bachelor*, but every spring out of nowhere there would appear a mate for her. Then they would pass on as they were all traveling men.

Maybe I can remember some of our cats' names. Tom was called *Tom Tittlemouse*. He was my main cat. Caroline's was a fine big tiger with a white face and throat, Croppie's oldest son. We called him *Tab Greengage Simply Him, Play the Drum Play the Drum*. Then there was *Dick Marmaduke Little, Play the Fiddle Play the Fiddle*. He was yellow, and also mine. And there was *Polly, Stranger, Lesley, Rindy, Randy, and Shiney-top*—the last three being named for characters in a story we read in the children's section of the **Detroit Free Press**, our only newspaper. Then there were *Midget First* and *Second*, and the kitten we loved the most, *Smut*. She came by her name because she was nearly all-white with a black thumbprint on her nose. Much to our sorrow Smut and the two Midgets were short-lived. We had a cat graveyard in the garden, where we planted wild-flowers, and we surely did suffer over the deaths of these loved pets.

Croppie's daughter was to be a mother, and Croppie tried to help when the kittens were born. It may not be usual for a mother animal to look after her young when they were grown, but she always did.

I happened upon a little scene on a warm summer's day, a nice nest under the big wild rosebush, and Polly and her new family, with old Croppie as busy as any grandmother helping to wash up the babies. Dear old Croppie. She was with us nearly all of our stay on the Divide. But it was one June day that we missed her, and it was nearly two weeks later that Mama found her dead in the tall grass a short way from the house.

In stormy weather the cats had to be carried to the barn at night, for every door and window in all the buildings had to be closed against the fine drifting snow. Bushels would come through a keyhole. So the last thing, after all the stock were fed and watered, some of us would have to put the cats on sacks and lug them through the snowdrifts to the barn. But in the morning they didn't have to be carried back as they would come running, smelling like hay and the cold clean outdoors! In our mile-high country the air was so pure that their fur was always clean and fresh, and there were never any fleas on our cats.

In the first year on our ranch we acquired a small black dog named Minnie, who sucked eggs. A lot of things were tried to break her of this, like giving her an egg that was full of red pepper, but to no avail. One day a man came along. He had young shepherd dogs, black and brown, with the most beautiful brown eyes a dog ever had. The man said he was in sheep, and had tried to train a dog named Rover to herd them, but he just wouldn't learn. So would we trade dogs? Of course we would! Yes indeed, for we wanted to get rid of Minnie and her appetite for eggs. So the trade was made, and Rover became our best-loved companion and friend throughout our childhood.

Rover had long silky hair, a bushy tail, and was fat and kind. The cats would sit on him as he lay before the fire in the winter. We never had to shut him up or scold him back if we didn't want him to go with us. When we were leaving he would follow us to the gate and look up with imploring eyes. If he were to stay, one had only to point toward the house and he would drop his head and sadly go back. But, if we wanted him to go with us, we would say, "You can come." Then what frisking and jumping to show his joy!

As long as he lived he hated sheepmen, and would go and hide if one came on the place. We thought he must have been treated cruelly by his former owner.

Rover always let the cats eat first. At milking time, twice a day, all the cats gathered around their big pan and drank their fill of the warm, rich, foamy milk. Rover would sit nearby, nose pointed away from the lapping cats, but with one eye kept on them. As soon as all had finished he would eagerly go forward for his share. And it was always forthcoming, for, as Mama said, he earned it if anyone did, helping with the bringing home of the cows.

Among other pets, I had a blue hen that spring. There were times when we saw flocks of blue grouse feeding with our chickens. Later, when the little new chicks were hatched, there were some that didn't look like Plymouth Rocks. They were sort of blue and had short legs. One, I thought cuter than the rest, I made a pet of. She was so tame I would pick her up and carry her around under one arm when gathering eggs in the barn. I was always a little afraid at dusk and it was a comfort to have something alive with me. Hecate, pronounced *Hackata*, was the name I gave her, and we talked together. I would call, "Hecate, Hecate — Hecate, good hen," and she would answer, "Hack, hack, hack," and come to me. She had one trait of the wild as she refused to lay her eggs in the nests in the chicken house. Instead she would choose a hide-out where we couldn't find her, and eventually she would appear proudly leading a flock of little chicks to show us. She was always a nuisance, as she wanted her family to live in the house with us, but we all loved her anyhow as she was so friendly.

It was during harvest that I missed Hecate. "Mama, Hecate is gone." I was in tears.

"Don't cry, dear. You know how she hides out when she is setting. She will come in when she gets good and hungry."

In spite of all of Mama's assurances, I went calling and looking, but there was no sign of Hecate, dear friend.

Two weeks went by and I was very sad. One day I went past the log haybarn, and out of habit was calling, "Hecate—Hecate, good hen." When I heard a thin, weak little "Hack...hack...hack." I could hardly believe my ears. I looked all around, then through a small opening between the logs I could see a little shining eye! I called to her, "I'm coming, Hecate, good hen."

This end of the big haybarn had no shed, as it was where the hauled hay was thrown through a large window. I didn't wait to go around through the shed door to where there was a ladder to the haymow. I had often climbed the log wall and sat in the high opening, and that was the way I went. It was quite a drop to the hay below, but I was in a hurry. Papa had hauled only one load of hay, just to feed the teams during harvest, and that was lucky for Hecate. She had found a nice hide-out where a plank leaned against the logs, making a small sheltered place for her nest. She must have laid a good many eggs before the men threw the load of hay in on top of her, for her nest was full of eggshells. She had eaten her own eggs which saved her life.

How I worked pitching the hay off the corner where she was! I worked and cried and sweated. Finally, I reached the plank and Hecate. I lifted her and she was so light, just bones and feathers. I don't know how I climbed out with Hecate under one arm, but I did and ran to the house calling, "Mama, Mama, here is Hecate, starving!"

Mama said, "Give her a little water first, then some moist bread. I think she'll be all right. Gracious, child, stop crying, now she is found!"

Day by Day

Papa often read aloud to us in the evenings. The first story I remember was *Millionaire Tommy*, about a bootblack who became rich, and married the beautiful blond girl. We heard *Uncle Tom's White Child*, and a lot of stories by Charlotte W. Bream. These, I believe, were in the *New York Ledger*. From the *Detroit Free Press* my father delighted to read M. Quand's *Bowers*. In that paper appeared Eugene Field's poems, *Little Boy Blue*, and the like. We loved to play out these stories, using our dolls or cats for actors.

Mama always knitted while Papa read to us. She made all our stockings for winter, and when the foot of a stocking was worn out she raveled it out and knit a new one.

Although our log cabin was new and finished in every way that was possible without money, and we had plenty of good food, as a kindly neighbor plowed us a garden which we planted with carefully hoarded seeds that Mama had brought from Missouri, we needed money for our winter supplies, and perhaps a cow and chickens. So, the first few years Papa would go outside the area and work during the summer.

This was to be his first time out, and as he prepared to leave for the new mining town of Cornucopia which lay on the south side of the Eagle Mountains, he promised, "When I come back I'll bring you each a big silver dollar."

With tears in our eyes we kissed him goodbye. Oh! How we would miss him and wait for his return.

While Papa was away Mama was not idle. She borrowed *range* cows from our neighbors who were glad to have them cared for in exchange for the milk the calves didn't need. She made butter and packed it in brine for selling in the fall when butter was scarce. Then there were huckleberries to pick, can, and dry. And amongst countless other chores the vegetables from our garden had to be harvested and stored in the double-log cellar that Uncle Jeff had helped Papa build.

From our one window the great snow-capped mountains could be seen. I used to sit on my little stool for hours at a time, looking at the mountains, and wondering where Papa was. As the time for his return drew near I picked out a little black speck on the mountainside that I thought might be him. Day after day I sat there, even into the evening, with my eyes glued on that speck, but it never got any nearer.

At last, one beautiful fall day when we were all in the cabin, who should come right into the room through the window but our gay young father! He had been too eager to go around the house to the door. Oh, what a welcome we gave him! I can still see the sweet look in my mother's eyes when she looked at him.

That evening, much to Caroline's and my joy, he gave us the promised silver dollars. Then we gathered in front of the big log fire and he told us of all his summer's adventures, of the odd people he had met, and their strange stories. And then, the climax of that wonderful day, he sang us a new song he had learned, *Sweet Dreamland Faces*. I have no way to tell of the deep, sweet joy that song brought us. Of course there were parts I did not understand, one line especially—*And with my Darling 'neath the Old Oak Stand.*

We had a stand-table, made by Papa, and Caroline and I often draped the big red and black shawl over it and pretended it was a cave where we hid from the Indians. So for many years I had a vision of two lovers sitting 'neath our old oak stand, peering out through the fringe of the red and black shawl.

After a few years Papa had enough money to buy our own animals. There were cows and calves, and nice fat black pigs. Then Papa built a big log barn because he didn't want our stock out in the bad weather like most ranches, but it meant lots of work to take the animals out, clean the stalls, chop the ice out of the trough in winter, and draw water for them. All of our stock were named and well cared for. Each cow knew just where to go to her place in the barn.

After getting the stock we were in need of a smokehouse. So one fall Papa started to build one out of logs, and before it was finished the nails ran out. He was in great fear of winter coming on before it was completed, and it was eighteen miles to town over terrible roads. So Mother took the hammer and walked nearly two miles to a deserted cabin and pulled out from it enough nails for my father to finish the building.

Papa also bought a team, Flax and Jude, a brood mare called Old Nell, and an old black Texas pony named Coalie. Coalie was old when we got her for riding to school on, but after she was twenty years old she had a nice black colt for us. We named the colt Topsy, and she was to be mine. How proud I was of her!

One early spring morning after breakfast Papa said, "Children, I am sorry to tell you that your cat Polly is dead. I found her in the horse manger when I was feeding. I think the frost is out of the ground enough so I can dig a grave for her in the cat graveyard."

Mama spoke up with, "While he is digging the grave you girls can take the egg basket and the big iron spoon and go over on the south hillside and dig up some flowers to set out on all the graves." That gave us something to do, so we wouldn't cry so hard. Mama and Papa were always so thoughtful.

So off we went to get the flowers, almost happy, for we loved to gather them after the long winter. By the time we returned with the little basket full of the sweet-smelling plants, Papa had Polly buried, and the other four cat graves rounded up with fresh dirt. After the flowers were all set out they looked so pretty that we felt quite proud of our work. But Caroline wasn't satisfied yet. "We don't know any songs for funerals," she said, "but I think we should sing something." So, after going through all the songs we knew, we decided that *Put My Little Shoes Away*, and *Nellie Gray* were the most suitable for the occasion. So there we stood, two little girls beside our cat's graves, singing our songs.

Then Mama came to the window and called us to dinner, an extra-nice dinner of sausage that had been stuffed into long cloth bags and smoked with the hams and bacon. When sliced it was round and about three inches across. Mama browned it on both sides, and made milk gravy to eat with the hot biscuits and baked potatoes. For dessert she had baked a big pie from gooseberries she had canned. Oh, that dinner was so good.

So our sorrows were forgotten, although we did miss Polly for a long time to come.

Steve was now twenty-one and could file on his homestead. Also he had received his share of his father's estate, several hundred dollars, enough to buy a good team of young geldings named Ben and Dave. We were all so proud of them, and the shiny new black harness and handsome wagon. I believe there had been enough left over to get farm machinery—a plow, harrow, and a wide rake for hay making. Papa's span of young mares, Flax and Jude, were not yet fully broken, so Steve's team was a great big help until ours were trained.

That summer, before one noon dinner, my father was washing up at the shelf in the kitchen where the water bucket, washpan, and handsoap were kept. As he dried his face and hands on the rough towel, made from a salt sack by my mother, he told her of his ride that morning, looking over the nearby countryside to see if what he had heard was true; namely that all the streams were dry, or nearly so. "Hashbrook, Two-Buck, and Three-Buck are all dry," he said. "We will have to water all the cattle from our spring and well. So be careful and don't waste any. There are no two ways about it, we are all going to starve out!"

After awhile the water-dogs appeared, coming from no telling what distance, and taking up quarters in our cherished spring. What a battle was waged against them, and what a task it was to destroy their eggs, even when the dogs themselves were all killed! One morning, when my mother went to put on her stockings, there was even a water-dog in one of them!

That year Mama dried a lot of huckleberries. They were wonderful in cookies, cakes, and puddings, but it had been such a good berry season that she was nearly out of sugar. Grandma was visiting us, and Mama said to her, "I am going to take ten gallons of berries to town and trade them for sugar." So Papa rigged the packsaddle on one of the horses, with two five gallon oil cans on each side, and away she went.

It didn't seem that she had been gone very long before we heard Rover bark, signaling that someone was coming. There was Mama with a real satisfied look, as she had returned with fifty pounds of granulated sugar.

The next summer Papa worked in harvest for three bushels of wheat per day, valued at twenty-five cents a bushel, but he got enough grain to grind to last us for a year.

Mama kept busy all summer long harvesting, canning, and drying fruits and vegtables for storing in our cellar for our winter food supply.

The cellar was a double-log frame, packed solid with dry earth between the logs. There were logs over the top, and that was heaped up with dirt and finished with well-fitted sod. Papa planted some grass seed also, so in the spring it was a solid green mound. There were two doors, one in each section of logs. In the winter Mama went in only when it was necessary to get vegetables, apples, and canned fruit. She had an old iron pot in which she carried hot coals into the cellar. The pot was left there to heat up the cold air that had come in when the door was opened, that way nothing ever froze.

Late in the fall of the year Mama went into the cellar to put away some canned prunes which Papa had got from the Reavis orchards on the alder slope above Enterprise. What met her eyes was appalling. The long shelf reaching from one end of the building to the other had pulled loose from what the men had thought were ample braces. There on the floor was lying, in ruin, all of the canned fruit she had worked on all the summer.

She came in looking white and terrible, walked over to the mantel, put her arms on it, hid her face, and began to sob. It was the first time we ever saw her cry and it scared us. Steve was there, and he found out what had happened. He said, "Cuss, Jinks, but don't cry!" He helped to clean up the fruit and broken glass, dug a deep hole between the big wild rose bush and the fence, and buried it deep, so no one would get hurt from the glass.

Mama said, "Well, I am glad I dried so many berries. We also have twenty gallons of preserves, five gallons each of peaches, green gages, pears, huckleberries, and prunes. Joe will have to buy more apples than usual, and we will get along."

Steve replied, "You are being brave now, Jinks, but I still think it would have helped if you could have cussed a little."

In early spring Grandma received a sad letter from Aunt Lou, saying, "Tommy has gone to his reward," and asking Grandma and Allie to come and spend a year with her. She would pay all expenses and provide Allie with good clothes for school. The family gathered together and talked it over, and as Grandma and Allie wanted so much to go it was decided that they should accept the invitation. Besides, Steve was building a new house, and the old one was hardly fit to live in. Steve could eat with us, and Mama would wash and mend for him. He said, "I'd rather sleep at the old house and have part of my meals there. It would save time when I am working at the building."

So Mama made Grandma and Allie each a dress for the trip. Around the end of May Steve planned to take them to the train so he was glad he had the new team and wagon as it was a ninety-five mile trek to La Grande.

After seeing Grandma and Allie safely on the train, and taking a short rest, he headed the team back home.

Upon his return he had a big load of lovely apples from the Grande Ronde Valley, but we were even more pleased with a picture-book apiece that Grandma had sent back to us. Caroline's was *Aladdin* and mine was *Blue Beard*. How we did adore them!

One day Mama was deeply disturbed to find a deck of playing cards in Uncle Steve's denim pocket when she went to wash his clothes. On top of that, he was also using white handkerchiefs with perfume on them!

"I wouldn't worry about him," said Papa. "There's no harm if the neighbor boys occasionally come over for a game with him. And remember, he is sparking Tressie, and wants to smell pretty."

A few days later Papa rushed in saying, "Jennie, one of the bulls gored Coalie in the shoulder, there is a flap of skin hanging that should be sewn back, can you do it?" Mama said, "I can try, if you and Steve can hold her." So Mama got out a long needle and some white thread, and went to the barn where Papa and Steve were standing, one on each side of Coalie.

Mama walked right up and said, "Good girl, stand still." Coalie seemed to understand, for she made no fuss—just shivered when Mama cleaned the wound with carbolic acid and warm water. There had to be a good many stitches taken, then the torn part covered well with turpentine and lard so the flies wouldn't get into it. After a few days Coalie could be turned out into the barn lot, and we were all proud of Mama.

Only a day or so later Papa came in with one of the hens. She was all swollen up in her neck and breast. "Look, Jennie, can you operate on this hen? She has eaten too much bearded barley, and it is all swollen up in her crop. She is choking to death."

Mama got out her little scissors, needle, and thread. Papa held the hen and Mama clipped the feathers off over her craw. Then she cut the skin of the craw, and the barley just rolled out! Mama cleaned it out good and sewed up the slit. As soon as the hen hit the ground she went to eating the grain that Mama had just taken out of her!

"This is a lesson to me," said Papa as he gathered up the grain to burn, "no more bearded barley on this place. There is a new kind called *bald* barley. That is what I shall plant next year."

47

One evening Papa and Mama came in after their work was done. "There is no two ways about it, Jennie, if it don't warm up soon we are going to starve out," Papa said with discouragement. It was cold and clear and looked as though there would be a frost. The oats and potatoes were looking fine but a frost would surely kill them.

"Let's not worry," Mama replied soothingly. "Things will work out somehow, and we'll manage." It was evening, all the chores were done, and we were gathered in front of the big fireplace with its bright log fire, ready for Papa to read to us. Mama had already started her knitting. Caroline and I had pulled out the stand-table from the corner, arranged the book, then the lamp with its polished chimney, a plate with four apples and a knife. We were waiting eagerly, for tonight the book was *Great Expectations*.

Caroline, sitting in her little rocking chair, asked, "Are we going to read tonight? I want to hear about Pip's going to play at Miss Haversham's."

"All right," Papa said, "I might as well read as set here and snuff ashes. If Mammy will light the lamp we'll begin." The oil lamp made a good light and we used it only for reading as oil was very expensive.

When Papa closed the book and laid it down the reading was over for the evening. I said, "Wish I could go some place like Pip did. I'm lonesome to see someone. I wish Grandma and Allie would come back from Missouri so we'd have someone to talk to."

"Well," said Mama. "How would you like to walk down and see the Huffmans? You could go after dinner tomorrow and come back after dinner the next day. You are ten years old, going on eleven, and I think you are old enough to go alone, so if it's a good day tomorrow you may go."

I was too excited to sleep that night, but I didn't forget when I said my "Now I lay me down to sleep" to ask God not to let the frost kill the crops lest we *starve out*. Always, as long as we lived on the ranch I continued to pray nightly that we would not starve to death. And God must have heard me, for the wind came up during the night and blew the frost away.

The next day was lovely and I was very busy all morning. I carried buckets of water from the spring, and Mama heated it in the wash boiler. Then the little washtub was brought into the kitchen and I took a bath in front of the kitchen stove, with the oven door open for heat. Afterwards I put my woolen stockings back on as Mama decided it wasn't warm enough yet to go without them. I was to wear one of my two new gingham dresses that Mama had just made for me and, to my delight, my new red flannel petticoat that was finished with red yarn lace knitted by my grandmother. To top it off I wore a pretty new chambray sunbonnet, in a lovely pink. I carried my little school lunch-bucket which contained my nightgown and fringed woolen shawl in case I got cold.

As we ate dinner I felt a little sad to be leaving Papa, Mama, Caroline, Rover, the new colt, and several new calves, not to mention our cats and Croppie's three new kittens who were just getting their eyes opened.

"Now be sure and tell the Huffmans that we will come and see them as soon as the spring work is done," Mama instructed me. After our noon dinner I set forth on my journey of two and a half miles to the Huffmans, feeling very proud and grown-up.

From our ranch on the ridgetop I had to walk about a half a mile before I started down the gulch. There were lots of trees, and after the bright sunshine it looked dark and gloomy. But I got used to it after a bit, and was soon enjoying the spring flowers and shrubs. The trail was fairly good for walking, but both sides were steep. The north side had lots of trees, but the south side was rim rocks and grass. There was a large hollow tree close to the trail. People had camped there and built fires in the hollow so that it was black and charred. As I drew near I saw what looked like an animal lying in front of the tree a short way from the hollow.

I wasn't sure what it was, but thought it was a wolf. I was very frightened and didn't know just what to do. To turn and go back home and have to say I was afraid would be terrible. There was no way around so I thought if I went past very quietly perhaps the animal would not hurt me. I went tip-toeing along, hardly breathing, and lo and behold, when I got closer I realized that it wasn't a wolf at all, or any other animal—just a pile of stones! So I made good time the rest of the way and didn't linger to pick flowers.

Soon I came to a little stream which the Huffmans used for drinking water. There was a little log culvert across it and when I walked over, the Huffmans' dogs heard me and came out barking. Right behind them came the children, and when they saw me they shouted back to their mother, "It's Daisy! It's Daisy, come to see us!"

The Huffman ranch was in a narrow bottom along Big Sheep Creek. The land was very rich, and they had far less cold and snow than we did on top. They even had a small orchard of crab apples, greengage plums, and prunes.

Mr. and Mrs. Huffman came out to greet me. Mrs. Huffman was a tall, lovely, kind-looking woman with dark blond hair. Mr. Huffman had red hair and very dark blue, twinkling eyes.

"Did you come all alone, Daisy?" Mrs. Huffman inquired.

"Yes," I answered proudly, "it isn't far and I'm going on eleven."

Mr. Huffman asked, "Well, how are the crops looking on top?"

Feeling all grown up to be discussing crops, I replied, "Well, not so good, Mr. Huffman. Last night Papa told Mama if it didn't warm up soon we sure would starve out."

"Now don't you worry, Daisy," said Mr. Huffman. "You folks have come through the winter in fine shape, and your papa didn't mean that you would go hungry—just that if the crops fail he might have to move out and go where there was work."

This was a long speech for Mr. Huffman, who had a soft voice and said very little. Papa once said that the reason John Huffman spoke so softly was that he was always afraid of waking the baby. I felt relieved at his words, but just the same, resolved to continue praying that we wouldn't *starve out*.

There were seven children in the Huffman family at that time. Arnold, the eldest, was a little older than me. He was a real pretty boy with dark waving hair and the deep blue eyes that all the Huffmans had. He was sensitive and cried easily, and for that reason the big boys at school teased him. None of them were as good-looking as Arnold, so they had to get even somehow. Sydney was a jolly girl, not pretty then, but later she was handsome like her mother. Lester was a good boy, soft-spoken and redheaded like his father. Victor was rather small, and not so pretty, but he was smart. And Welthy was a darling. She was named for the daughter of one of our neighbors, and I always loved her. At school, when we played house, she was my little girl. She had really golden hair, *the* blue eyes, and lovely skin. Mary was next to the baby, very cute and round. The baby, several months old, was named Johnora, and I was allowed to hold her, much to my delight. How I longed for a baby like her!

Their home was a double log house with an enclosed connecting passageway between the large living quarters and the smaller cabin used for kitchen and dining-room. There was a small bedroom on one side of the living room for company. It was also used by Mrs. Huffman in cold weather when she had a new baby. The living room was heated by a large stove, and the stovepipe going to the upstairs gave it some of the heat.

The kitchen cabin had a huge cookstove, and a long table to eat on, with long benches on each side of it. The upstairs room had two rows of beds, one side for the boys and the other for the girls and their grandmother. I think Mr. and Mrs. Huffman usually slept on the boys' side, but the night I was there they and the baby slept in the downstairs bedroom.

The grandmother was always a mystery to me. I saw her many times but was never able to see her face, for she always wore a black calico sunbonnet. I wondered if she wore it to bed, but I never found out, for she blew out her candle before undressing.

After my long walk I was quite hungry, and the supper surely looked good. There were platters of cold sliced venison and hot sourdough biscuits. Mrs. Huffman was a good gardener so there were lots of vegetables, especially big raw sliced onions. We never had such big sweet onions as the ones grown in the soil along the creek bottom. There was lots of cold milk for us children, and strong boiled green tea for the grownups.

After Sydney and I had helped with the dishes we children played *Button. Button. Who's got the button?* We also tried to play *Drop the Handkerchief,* but the room was too crowded.

Bedtime came early and at eight o'clock we girls went first so we could get ready for bed before the boys came up. People slept with their underclothes on then, but our family always wore nightgowns besides. However, the Huffman children didn't bother with them; perhaps they didn't have any. My red petticoat and long handknit stockings were much admired, but I heard the grandmother remark, "I don't hold with pampering children!" And later, when I asked my mother what she had meant, my mother evaded the question.

There was a waterfall near the house, and the noise of the water rushing and tumbling down it, combined with the fact that I slept with Sydney who was a *kicker,* kept me awake most of the night. I was really black-and-blue the next morning, but I was careful not to let her see, for I did not want to hurt her feelings. All of the Huffman children went barefoot most of the time, so their feet were hard and rough.

I don't recall how, or if, we all got washed for breakfast, but I do remember the huge roller towel, and the big tin pan for all to wash in. The family comb was tied with a string to a nail on the wall so it wouldn't get lost. People always used to use the same comb and it would have been an insult to take your own comb when visiting. We children all wore our hair short, so it didn't make much difference whether it was combed or not.

We had a good breakfast of eggs, biscuits, molasses, and delicious brown ham gravy, the best ever made anywhere. After breakfast, it being Sunday, Mrs. Huffman took the big iron teakettle full of hot water into the living-room, put it on the heating stove to keep warm, got the wash-pan, a bar of yellow soap, a washcloth and towels, and all the children got their necks and ears washed good, whether they needed it or not. And afterwards, to my amusement, the girls got the fronts of their brown denim dresses washed off, and then were made to stand in front of the stove until dry!

Mrs. Huffman remarked, "I have found that denim dresses for the girls, as well as shorts and overalls of denim for the boys, save a lot of washing. They can wear them all winter."

When Sydney and Welthy were all washed and dried they asked me to go upstairs with them to see their *pretty things*. For a place to keep the girls' treasures Mrs. Huffman had partitioned off a corner of the bedroom with an old sheet. The boys and little children were not allowed to touch anything there. I expected to see a box of colored picture cards, a button *charm-string*, or some dolls; things such as Caroline and I had, but I got a surprise. We all knew that Mrs. Huffman was in the habit of sending off for brass jewelry, but we had never seen her wear any of it. And now I discovered that each of the two older girls had a lovely plush jewel-case with lots of wonderful jewelry — watches, lockets, rings, breast-pins, and more things than I can remember, plus some pretty silk handkerchiefs.

But the biggest surprise of all came when Sydney carefully unrolled from many layers of perfumed tissue paper and cotton a big, white, ostrich-feather fan, beautifully clean! I was speechless with admiration, although at that time I didn't really understand Mrs. Huffman's longing for beautiful things, and her desire to give her children something more than food and shelter.

"Don't you have any dolls?" I asked.

Sydney answered, "We did have at Christmas, but dolls don't last very long around here. The kids soon tear them up. Do you still have your doll Louisiana?"

"Yes", I replied, "but you are saying her name Louisiana. It's Anna Louise, but the way you say it is nice, too."

"Where did you get Anna Louise?" asked Sydney, and I answered, "A lady down at Enterprise had thrown the head out on the trash heap. I asked if I could have it and she said, "Sure, but the head is broken off so short that it can't be fastened to a body. That doll was brought across the plains in a covered wagon when I was a little girl. I hope your mother can fix it for you somehow."

"So I took the doll-head home, and Mama said she thought she could fix it. She melted some pitch from the pine trees, filled the doll-head with it, stuck a good strong stick into it, and let it harden. Then she made a doll's body and stuffed it with sawdust, sharpened the end of the stick and forced it down into the sawdust body. And finally she wound wide cotton tape around the doll's neck and sewed it to the body."

And now Mrs. Huffman called us to dinner. "Well, what did you think of the girls' *pretty things*?" She asked me. I answered that they were all very pretty but that I liked the fan best of all. In fact, I longed to stay upstairs with the fan, and just hold it in my arms.

Dinner was grand—a pot of venison, a huge platter of boiled potatoes, sliced onions, creamed carrots, biscuits, and what looked like a gallon of gravy. Did you ever eat dried peaches, stewed and served with good rich cream? And there was warm spice cake to go with the peaches. Mrs. Huffman was famous for her spice cakes. We always looked for her cake at school picnics and Fourth of July gatherings.

Before I started home Arnold gave me a little gadget just about half as long as my little finger and about the same size around. You could shut one eye and look through one end, and there was the Lord's prayer, magnified so that it was easy to read. It seemed wonderful that so small a thing could hold so much.

The children all begged their mother to let them go part of the way with me. I was polite and told Mrs. Huffman, "Thank you for a nice time." I then invited them all to come see us, and they said, "Come again."

"You can all go as far as Papa's stack of new fence rails. That's far enough," said Mrs. Huffman, "Mary will be tired and want someone to pack her." We raced over the culvert, but had to stop, for Mary already wanted to be carried. I said, "Let me pack her now, for you all will have to get her home." So even though she was quite a load I loved the feel of her soft little body. Mary carried my basket, and all too soon we came to the pile of rails and they had to turn back. Oh! How I wished they could have come as far as the *wolf tree*. I hurried past it, not even looking at the spot where I thought the wolf lay.

Just before I reached the top I paused long enough to put the little shawl about my shoulders, and pinned it up close about my neck, as Mama had told me, for she said, "You will be warm walking the gulch, and the wind will feel cold when you reach the top." I was glad for the shawl, and thought how Mama was always right.

I had a mile to walk before I could see our barn, then the house. How comfortable it all looked! Then came Rover with welcoming bark. Papa was just coming out the gate, he gave me a hug and said, "I'm glad our big girl is home again." There were Mama and Caroline smiling in the doorway, and even the cats seemed glad to see me.

It was evening chore-time and Mama always helped with the milking. The milk had to be strained and set on a shelf in the spring house, and then supper had to be eaten and cleared away before I could tell about my visit. To welcome me home we had my very favorite meat — sugar-cured round of beef that was cooked over hot coals raked from the fireplace. The Dutch oven which we brought from Missouri was heated very hot, and thin slices of the meat were broiled in it to a delicate brown on both sides, seasoned with salt and pepper with a chunk of butter added. There were fresh, light bread, cucumber pickles, and, much to my joy, a green gooseberry pie served with thick sweet cream. I enjoyed the food at the Huffmans, but after all, Mama's cooking couldn't be beaten.

Before supper I asked Caroline, "Did Papa read last night?"

"No," she answered, "but we popped corn, and had the last of the apples, but we saved one for you. We also sang songs, and Mama and Papa told stories about their childhood back in Missouri."

Coming from Missouri, and having been used to corn in all its forms—hominy, cornbread, popcorn, et cetera—we longed for it more than one could imagine, so I was sorry to have missed out on the popcorn. I think it was the second winter on our new ranch that I remember my mother got out her seed sack and said there was no use keeping the seed corn as we couldn't raise corn on our ranch. So she took the little bags, so carefully made in Missouri and filled with the best kinds of corn to be planted in the new country, and emptied them into a large, thick skillet with butter and salt. She raked some hot coals forward onto the hearth, set the skillet on them, and thus parched us a mess of popcorn—I can still remember how good it was!

Later I told Caroline she could have my apple.

"No," she answered, "we'll cut it in two and share it."

Then we planned a picnic for the next day, if it was warm enough. We would go to our rock castle on the south hillside. With the apple and some bread and jelly we could have a lunch, and pick some buttercups.

Finally, after the dishes were done we all gathered around the fire and Mama asked, "Did you have a good time? Is the baby as pretty as Mary?" So I told all the news about the Huffman family, just what we had to eat, how cute the baby was, and how Mary could talk. I saved for the last what was the most important to me—about the girls' *pretties*.

I said, "They have a lot of chains, rings, lockets, and silk handkerchiefs." Then I described the white feather fan, how soft and pretty it was, and how it had perfume on it!

Mama said, "But what use can it be? There's no place to use it in this country!"

I replied that it looked like the picture in my story book showing Cinderella with the fan she took to the ball.

Mama was looking at me as I talked and I thought she looked different somehow, but we didn't say any more about the fan then. I had a feeling that she didn't care to hear any more about it. But I had Caroline for an audience later, and she loved to hear about the lovely white fan. That is when I wished that Arnold had sent the trinket to Caroline, as she thought it was so nice.

One day in October we heard Rover give his welcome bark, and when we looked out, there were Mrs. Huffman and Sydney at the corral gate. They were riding Old John, their gentle, fat, family riding horse. The children rode him to school, as many as could stick on, and he didn't mind. I ran out to open the gate and welcome them, saying, "I'll give Old John a drink before I put him in the barn." "Would you like to ride him down to the spring branch?" asked Mrs. Huffman. "Oh, yes," I said, so they boosted me up on his back, and how high up I felt! Our riding horses were not nearly so tall. After his drink Sydney and I took the blanket and surcingle off, also the bridle, so he could eat comfortably. I climbed into the hay barn and threw down some good oat hay. One of the most important rules to learn in stock country is to care for your horse before doing anything else.

When we got to the house I saw that Mama was making some custard pies, and I was glad. We had lots of milk and eggs and she made them rich and thick, with lots of grated nutmeg on top. There had been a big black iron pot of large red beans and a ham shank simmering on the cookstove all morning, for Papa and Steve had gone to the timber for a load of wood, and Mama wanted a good dinner for them when they returned. After the pies were done she had ready for the oven a big long pan of graham bread with fresh pork cracklings stirred into it. We folks from Missouri missed our cornbread, but made out with graham. Then there was a big dish of raw sauerkraut. Besides the pies for dessert there were cookies, jam, and jelly.

By the time Papa and Steve came everything was ready, and everyone enjoyed the good food, especially Sydney. As soon as dinner was over and the dishes washed, we asked Sydney if she would like to play outside. "No," she replied, "I'd rather stay in the front room and look at your doll-house."

Then I realized that she was too full to walk very much, so we sat on the rag rug before the doll-house. Caroline and I had made the house from two orange crates resting on their sides, one on top of the other. This made an upstairs with two bedrooms, and a downstairs with a kitchen and front room. We used cigar boxes for bedsteads, with little pieced quilts and pillows, and little rag rugs for the floor. A black tin can that had held concentrated lye made a good stove, with a round stick for a stovepipe.

Caroline and I had made the dolls that lived in this house. Each of us had a Mama and Papa doll with several children. They were all rag dolls, but looked cute in the clothes we had made for them. We even made cats of white cotton flannel by rolling up a little piece of cloth, and winding a thread very tightly around one end for a head. The other end had a tail, and the face would have black thread knots for eyes and thread whiskers.

Sydney was so interested that she didn't want to go home. She looked back longingly as they left the house, saying, "I wish we had a purty house." As Mrs. Huffman left she remarked to Mama, "Well, Jennie, I thought I better come see you while I could. I won't be getting out for quite awhile." "Oh!" said Mama, and I wondered at her answer.

After our company had gone I went into the front room and really looked at it for the first time. And I decided it was *purty*, just as Sydney had said. Mama had painted all the raw plank boards that formed the door, window casings, bedsteads, and stand-table a nice brown. There was a gay red print curtain in front of the beds, and they were always made up nicely with pillow shams, bolster-shams, and pretty piece quilts for bedspreads. There was a dresser with several shelves in it, which Papa had made from a large packing-case. Mama had put a white starched curtain, like a petticoat, around it, and a crocheted rag rug beside each bed. We had good beds. They had slats to put the straw ticks on, then the big featherbeds were put on the ticks, and finally, the bed-clothes. They looked wonderful when finished, but, sad to say, they did not stay puffed up once we were in bed.

The walls were freshly papered each spring with the carefully hoarded newspapers, and Mama would also cut them for scalloped paper shelf-covers. There were white starched window curtains, a clock, the chairs Grandpa Bunnell had made for us, and the stone fireplace that always looked nice and friendly, even when there wasn't a fire burning in it.

That evening I told Mama and Papa that Sydney had said she wished they had a purty house, adding, "And I think our house is purty, too." They looked very pleased.

In late fall, when the weather turned cold, Papa killed hogs. This year Mr. Huffman and Steve were to help him. Steve's hogs were to be butchered at our place, and later Papa and Steve would go down and help Mr. Huffman. Mama would send the Huffman family some spareribs and sausage. Papa asked Mama the day before the butchering if she could ride over to the Drumhill's and borrow their sausage machine. "I have another load of dry wood in the timber," he said, "and should get it before it is covered with snow."

"Of course I'll go," said Mama, "I haven't seen Mrs. Drumhill in a long time. I'll eat dinner with them and make a lunch for you to take with you. The children will be all right by themselves."

Papa left early, as it was quite a long way. Mama didn't go until all the work was done, and she had told us what to eat for our dinner. The Drumhills lived about eight miles away. There were few sausage machines on the Divide and they made the rounds during hog-killing time.

I had wanted to bake a cake all by myself for a long time. I had asked Mama but she always said, "Wait until you are older—there is plenty of time." But I wanted to do it now, so, almost before she was out of sight, I commenced to gather sugar, butter, eggs, and flour together. I guess I forgot the baking powder, but as I used a lot of eggs the cake did raise somewhat. But when I took it from the oven it *fell*.

Caroline and I were so disappointed. We had planned to surprise Mama and Papa with a cake for supper. As we stood looking sadly at the thin cake we heard someone step on the flat rock in front of the kitchen door. It was a rather rough-looking man with a pack on his back. He asked, "Where is your mother?"

I told him she wasn't at home. Then he said, "I would like very much to have something to eat. Could you fix me a bite?"

I said, "I can fry some eggs and bacon, also there is bread that Mama just baked. Will that do?"

"How about some coffee?" He asked.

"I never made any," I replied, "but if you can make it, all right."

"Sure," he said, and so together we got a nice dinner. I went to the spring-house for cream and butter, and there was lovely jelly and huckleberries.

I saw him looking at the cake, and I said, "I tried to bake a cake but it fell. Do you think you could eat a piece?"

" I sure can. I always have liked warm cake." And to my surprise he ate several pieces. He said he had come up from Mexico and was heading for the Seven Devils Mine. He had a little tobacco bag in his pocket which he emptied on the table. "They are opals," he said. "Each of you may have one." We were delighted, and I asked if he would like for me to fix him a lunch to take with him. "Yes, indeed," he answered, "that would be a big help. There are so few living in these mountains." So I made a good lunch for him, and was inspired to include the remainder of the sad cake. When he said good-bye he gave each of us a fifty cent piece—a lot of money in those days. And I got rid of my cake failure without Mama ever seeing it.

A short time after the man left, Mama came home. When we told her how we had had company for dinner she looked frightened and asked, "Was he a tramp?"

"Well, he gave each of us an opal to set in a ring, and fifty cents, but he had a pack on his back like a tramp."

Mama said, "Well, he must have been all right. Looks like you fed him well."

That evening Mama told Papa, "I stay here for months and no strangers come, then right away when I am gone a few hours, look what happens!"

Early in November Mama announced that she was going to town. "Now, Mammy, I think it is foolhardy for you to go. You know we always get our first big snow about this time of year," warned Papa.

"Not until the thirteenth," said Mama. "You know it generally comes on Caroline's birthday and this is only the eighth, so I will be safe."

"All right, all right," said Papa. "You always were bullheaded, but I want you to walk down the big hill. Coalie is old and stiff and might fall."

Mama promised also that she would walk up the hill, for Coalie would be packing quite a load on the return trip.

It was eighteen miles over mountain roads to Joseph. Mama would stay overnight with friends on Prairie Creek on her way home. We didn't have a sidesaddle and it wasn't seemly for a woman to ride *straddle*, so she used Papa's saddle. The horn was broken off which made it better for her. Papa removed the stirrup on the right side, and tied the large package of butter behind the saddle.

Mama wore a long denim riding skirt, warm jacket, fur cap and mittens, and before she put on these clothes she slipped into her long, high-necked nightgown and then put on her good wool dress. She said, "If it is very cold tonight, and if they don't have enough covers where I stay, I will still be warm when I go to bed."

When she was ready to go I thought she looked rather bulky, but to be warm was more important than looks. Like all ranchers at that time we turned our beef, hogs, butter, and eggs in to the store, and they furnished us with all the necessities during the year. Needless to say, they did not carry feather fans. We had plenty of credit at the General Merchandise Store, but Mama said, "I am going to take the sixteen pounds of butter I have made and sell it to Mrs. Mitchell at the hotel. She will give me cash, so I will have money for a little Christmas shopping."

After Mama left, Papa worked around the house, splitting stove-wood for winter. I helped him carry it into the *little* room, which was part pantry and part storage space. It was large enough so that it would hold enough dry wood for cooking all through the winter. Caroline even helped rick it up, but we both soon grew tired.

Mama always made six mince pies at a time in the winter, five of which she froze in the pantry. We also had a number of dressed chickens hanging in the spring house, frozen. It saved feeding them and they were all ready when we wanted chicken.

Papa split one of the chickens in half and put it into the oven to bake with the potatoes. Then after the chores were done he added a fat mince pie, so it was hot when we wanted it. Everything smelled so good that we could hardly wait to start the feast.

That evening, after a supper of cold chicken, bread and butter, jam, and glasses of cold milk, we begged Papa to tell one of our favorite stories of how he got lost when a little boy in Missouri. "All right," he began, "When I was about your age, Daisy, my Pa let me take the little squirrel gun and go hunting. It was grand fall weather, just right to hunt the squirrels, as they were nice and fat from feeding on acorns and other nuts. The woods in Missouri have lots of food for animals and birds, also for the wild razorback hogs. The foliage on trees and bushes was pretty and red, and I found a wild grape vine with a lot of dried grapes on it which I picked. I ate some, but put most of them in my game bag for my little sisters, Cora, Julie, and Kate. Then I gathered all the big fat *hicker* my bag and pockets would hold. Along the way I saw a big razorback sow with a litter of shoats. I even heard a wild turkey's gobble. I shot three big fat squirrels, and tied their hind legs together so I could carry them over a stick on my shoulder. I noticed it was getting late, and dusky in the timber, and decided it was about time I went home. I had a big load and was getting hungry. So I struck out in the direction I thought was right, but the longer I walked the more unfamiliar the surroundings looked. So I changed course, but that didn't look right either. Then I started to run, holding my gun carefully, and the bag of nuts kept hitting my legs. I ran *this-away* and *that-away* until I was petered out. Then I stopped and leaned against a tree to rest, and suddenly I saw a queer looking house and barn — they looked as if they were frowning at me. I remembered the stories the colored folks had told me about haunted houses and witches, so I hid behind the tree to see what would happen. The cabin door opened and a queer looking old woman with a shawl over her head came out with a pan of food, and called, 'Here, chick. Here, chick,' and it was Ma! I ran to her, crying, and she said, 'Why Joey, what is the matter?' I told her I had been lost and that even our house had scared me. 'Well, dress your squirrels and we will have supper,' she said, 'I know you're hungry. We have shortenin' bread and it will be good with the squirrels.' "

Mama reached home tired, but without mishaps. I thought how pretty she looked, with her cheeks all pink from being out in the cold. Papa noticed, too, and commented to Caroline and me, "Who is there as pretty and sweet as your Mommy?"

I have always remembered how happy we all were that evening. Mama brought with her many interesting packages, some of which were not to be opened until Christmas. She showed us a large package of chocolate for making candy and cake frosting, also shredded coconut in a tin box, some black tea, which I think was called *Spider Legs*, vanilla and lemon extract, and ground cinnamon. There was also nutmeg, which had to be grated on a little grater. And there was a little bag of nuts and hard candy, sent by the merchant with whom we did most of our trading.

"How did you fare last night?" Papa asked.

"I nearly froze! I kept on my basque when I went to bed, and tucked my wool dress-skirt around my feet. There was just one cotton comforter on the bed, the cotton was in lumps and you could see through it. It beats me how a man who has good barns for his horses, and good farm machinery, doesn't provide a better house and furniture for his family. His wife and children are so nice, too. I enjoyed seeing them."

"Well Mammy, you are safe home, and if we don't have any bad luck I think we are all fixed for winter. You have lots of canned fruit, and we have a bin of good apples, potatoes, cabbage, beets, rutabagas, turnips, carrots, dry onions, and parsnips. Besides, the smoke house is full of hams, bacon and sausage, head-cheese, and lard. And upstairs we have barrels of flour, sugar, rice and beans."

———————————————————

Just after Christmas the Bunnells asked Papa to come and help them butcher a beef. He knew how to cut it up so there would be no waste, and he could also show them how to sugar-cure parts, make corned beef, and other things.

Before he left, Mama told him to accept a quarter of the beef if it was offered, as we were nearly out of candles, and needed the tallow. So, Papa took the wagon just in case it should be offered.

We were all pleased when he came back that afternoon with a nice quarter of beef. Now we would have beefsteaks, roasts, and all the other good things Papa did with beef.

After the meat was all cut up and trimmed, Mama cut the suet up fine and heated it in a large pot to render it out. She poured the fat into milk pans, and after it was cold it could be turned out into large cakes of tallow.

Mama let Caroline and me make the candle wicks. She tore long, thin strips, like carpet rags, from an old sheet. We each held an end, and twisted. Sometimes one of us would accidentally let go, and then we would have to start all over again. We had to twist it until Mama said, "That is enough. Now fold it together and see how it twists up by itself."

Mama would mold thirty-six candles. Our candle-mold held only six, so it would be several days before they were all finished. The tin candle-mold had a small hole in the bottom of each section. Mama made a knot in the twisted wick end, and threaded it through the hole so it made a stopper to prevent the tallow from leaking through. The other end of the wick was tied to a stick long enough to reach across the top of the mold. Of course this had to be done to all six molds before the hot tallow was poured in. The wicks had to be tight, for a loose wick would make a poor candle.

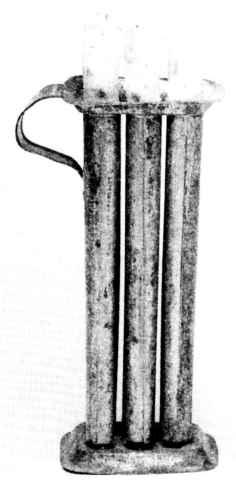

After Caroline and I had made six wicks and watched Mama's care and patience in getting them just right, Caroline said, "I don't like candles, nohow. They don't give enough light to read by."

"I know, dear," Mama said, "but we have to save the coal oil for Papa to read by. The candles do very well in the kitchen or when we are not reading. I can knit with my eyes shut, you know."

The snow started settling in and it stormed for days on end. Oftentimes the wind blew the snow so hard that it was impossible to see the barn, and we couldn't go outside. Before long the snow got so deep Papa had to start feeding the stock in the barn.

Stray horses kept coming around the place looking for something to eat, and Papa had to keep running them off.

The winter seemed to drag on, and we missed Grandma and Allie awfully bad since they left for Missouri the previous year.

No one came to see us as the snow was too deep. Papa and Steve could drive the team and the big bob-sled right over our railing fence tips whenever they fed the stock outside.

After the storm let up we cut five steps in our snow stairway to the top of the fence. The snow was nice and hard to play on with our sled, but we were not allowed to coast down the slopes, as Mama was afraid we would slide too fast and hurt ourselves.

Most days the stock would be able to go to the water trough near the well where Papa drew water for them by the bucketful. But sometimes the wind blew the snow so badly that they refused to go out, and they would just have to wait until the storm was over. But, the chickens never suffered as Mama always saw to it that there was plenty of warm water for them during these stormy periods.

Early in March we had a *chinook*. Papa was very uneasy, for he feared floods. In Missouri his family had lived on bottomland near Little Clear Creek, and every spring they had had a flood. Mama tried to reassure him. "Why Joe," she said, "we are on a mountain top."

"Yes, I know, but look at the six-foot snow banks all around us, and the chinook is making holes in them like you had thrown hot flatirons through them!"

During the night I was awakened by the sound of running water, and of Mama and Papa talking outside. I looked out and saw them working very fast, digging a ditch in the snow around the house. The water from the melting snow did not come into our house, but it would have if Papa had not kept watch and dug the ditch to carry it off while Mama held the lantern for him. Before morning it started to freeze, and for several days afterward the country around us was a glare of ice. People had to wrap their horses' legs in gunny sacks to keep the ice from cutting them. But this was the last of the bad winter, and not long after we began to see little bits of green grass sticking up through the snow. The first buttercup showed itself the first week of March—we knew then that spring was really coming at last.

Around the end of March Mr. Marr and his son Jess came by the ranch looking for their lost horses. They were the first visitors we had seen since the long winter began.

It wasn't long before the grass began greening pretty fast. But that brought out the ticks which kept us busy *ticking* the cattle and horses.

Steve planned to build a chicken house that spring, and decided to go up to the big timber and pick out the logs. It was too early to drive the wagon as the frost was still in the ground. It would melt during the day, and a wagon would be hard to get through the top mud, so he rode Snapper, his riding mare that he loved more than most anything. She was a pretty bay with white socks. He had trained her himself, and she seemed to understand just what he said to her.

We were surprised to see him return before noon. When he came in the house Mama was frightened to see that he had a big bruise on his forehead, and that his clothes were soaking wet. After he had put on dry garments Mama gave him a big cup of ginger tea laced with brandy and nutmeg. While he drank it he told us of his mishap.

"I was just riding along slow," he said, "the sun felt good on my back and I liked the scent of early spring in the timber. We came to a bridge of peeled poles, the stream was high from the snow melting in the mountains, and we were nearly across when Snapper's feet flew out from under her as she wasn't shod. That was the last I knew till I felt something pulling at me and licking my face. I found I was partly in the water, with my head and shoulders on the bank, and Snapper was trying her best to drag me up the embankment. Look at my jumper, where she had torn it with her teeth! She was licking my face, something I never saw a horse do, even to their colts! I tell you, Jinks, she saved my life, and I will keep her and care for her as long as she lives."

As it turned out, Snapper lived to be over twenty years old, with every comfort a horse could wish for.

Our cow Pinky was just two years old. She was to have an early calf, and Papa was watching her very closely. There was green grass on the south hillside, and he hated to keep her in the corral when she wanted to go with the other cattle to graze. The sun was nice and warm so he let her out. But toward the middle of the afternoon he felt uneasy and said to Mama, "Jennie, would you take Coalie and ride down a ways on the hillside and drive Pinky in? Take Rover to help you." Papa was busy mending fences and did not want to quit.

Mama did not bother to put a saddle on Coalie, but went out with just a blanket and surcingle. It was getting dark before she came home. We ran to meet her as Papa opened the corral gate to let Pinky and Coalie through. Then we saw that Mama was holding something in front of her. It was a tiny red calf.

"Mammy, how did you get that calf up on Coalie alone?" Papa asked.

"Well, when you've got to do something," replied Mama, "you just find a way to do it. Pinky wasn't with the other cattle and I went down the canyon looking for her. She was in among a bunch of little second-growth trees. I didn't dare go back for help for the coyotes would surely have killed the calf. It was too weak to stand, and so small that I thought I could get it onto Coalie. She rolled her eyes at me when I lifted it up on her. There was a big rock nearby. I led her, holding the calf, to where I could climb up on the rock, and somehow I managed to get on behind the calf, and here we are."

After the long winter everyone was busy—cleaning out the barn, mending fences, straightening up around the house, planting flowers, and tilling the garden.

We papered the kitchen, and smoked the sitting room with sulfur. Papa built some new fence, harrowed the field, and planted barley while Mama went to town to get us some books and shoes for school. Uncle Steve and Mr. Huffman worked on the schoolhouse to get ready for another year.

Grandma and Allie had just returned from Missouri after spending a year there, and we were thrilled to have them home again. Allie was now sixteen and had decided that she didn't want to go to to school anymore.

Papa and Steve had spent the past year building a large log house on Steve's claim. Mama remarked, "The way Steve is fixing up the new house it looks like he is thinking of getting married." And she smiled in a knowing sort of way.

It was wonderful to have our Grandmother and Aunt Allie home from Missouri. Allie was quite grown-up at sixteen, slim and pretty, but she still had her freckles, to my secret satisfaction. I was a chunky little girl, and she took delight in measuring my waist and hers to see how much larger around I was than she. But I did have a pink-and-white complexion and no freckles, so that was a comfort to me.

School on the Divide

Mama's Uncle Jeff taught the first school ever held between the Sheeps the summer of 1887, with about forty pupils, as I remember. He stayed at our house for the summer, and every morning I would ride with him on his pony, Blue Pod.

Uncle Jeff had the most musical speaking voice I have ever heard. He gave singing lessons one evening a week at the schoolhouse for local ranchers and their families, and the young men with their sweethearts. It was a social event and much enjoyed by all as there were so few occasions for people to get together back then.

The schoolhouse was pretty cramped with all of the pupils, and I remember that every Friday he would give out Reward of Merit cards. They had silk fringe around them, and some of them were perfumed—what joy to have them in one's box of picture cards. Each child then treasured all colored pictures and would show them to their friends along with their *charm strings*, and of course we knew where each one came from.

One thing stands out in my memory of that year. A homesteader near the schoolhouse had lost a baby girl, and Uncle Jeff in his impulsive way had decided that it would be fitting for the school children to call and view the body. Most of us had never seen a dead person and we started out as on a holiday. Uncle Jeff had us gather wildflowers along the way—there were so many and so lovely—and in this way we came to the little board shack, laden with pretty flowers. He had instructed us to pass the body in single file, and to place the flowers about her, which we did. The house was clean and bare, and all I noticed was the rough table with the beautiful little child all dressed in white, asleep, and the tall care-worn mother with her grim, resentful mouth and sad expression.

I was a very shy child, and even now I can remember the injustice shown me by my uncle in his efforts to be amusing. On my birthday, during school, he had me stand in front of the class with a tall paper duncecap on my head. After they all had their fun I was told that it was just a joke, because it was my birthday. I didn't care for Uncle Jeff's idea of fun.

But one joyful thing happened on my birthday—my little friend Bessie Sims told me that she had had a little sister born that day, and had been allowed to name her for me. That made me so proud and happy.

In 1890 school was to start about the middle of June, there were to be sixteen pupils, and each of us had to furnish our own desk. I remember that Papa had our neighbor, Grandpa Bunnell, build a wooden desk for us that year.

Our teacher's name was Lulu Coverdale, and to my great joy she boarded at our house that summer. She was such a bright-eyed pretty girl, only eighteen years old. It was her first teaching job, and she was eager to teach us not only the usual things, but also good manners—how to say "Excuse me," "Thank you," and so on. We all loved her, especially the big boys. Mama and Papa felt much safer to have her with Caroline and me, as we rode horseback to school, and Lu walked beside us the two and a half miles. Before Caroline had started to school the year before, I had always walked.

Caroline and I were in the same class, as there were no grades and our classes were decided by what reader we were in. We had the advantage of home teaching and our father's reading aloud to us. Some of the children didn't understand a story if Lu read it to the class.

Caroline and her friend Esther Brown spent their recess and noon hours sitting in a fence corner on the grass, trading songs. Before the short term of school was over they knew all the verses. I remember those that Esther traded to Caroline were all hillbilly songs from the mountains of Tennessee.

Once in a great while Rover was allowed to go with us to school. Our desk sat by one of the two windows of the schoolhouse, and when Rover went with us he would lie under the window outside so he could keep an eye on us. One day, when he had gone to school with us, our father rode past the schoolhouse, hunting for a stray cow, and he called Rover to help him. This was a Friday afternoon, and when we got home after school we didn't miss Rover until evening. And it was something to worry about, for he never left home without one of us. All day Saturday we wondered and called, and we feared that he had been killed or stolen. On Sunday it suddenly occurred to me that he might still be waiting for us at the schoolhouse. I got my pony and hurried over the two and a half miles distance. When I reached the top of the hill, and looked down at the schoolhouse I could see our dear, faithful friend sitting by the window, patiently waiting for us to come out and go home. He had helped my father drive the cow home and then had returned to wait for Caroline and me. We had been inside when he last saw us, so in his dog reasoning he felt he must wait until we came out. I got off my horse and hugged and kissed him. Then we hurried home to get him a lot of good things to eat.

The three months of school passed all too soon. We loved to have children to play with and we enjoyed the school work, all except for learning the multiplication tables. That got me, especially when Caroline learned them first. Lu, our teacher, told me one night when we had gone to bed, "Daisy, if you will learn the tables good before school is out, I will buy you a nice doll." I promised to try hard, and to my surprise I learned them before the close of school. Lu did so much for her pupils. Mother said when she was at the Huffman's house the children wore her out walking in front of her so they could say, "Please, excuse me," as Lu had taught them to do.

School lasted until the middle of September. We all loved Lu as our teacher and we were sorry to say good-bye. To our surprise and delight, though, we found out that she would again be our teacher the coming year.

We were to have a new teacher, a man named Mr. Crow, for the summer of 1895, and he was to board with us. Nearly everyone was anxious for school to start that year because of the very long winter.

The first day of school was on the 13th of May, but only thirteen children showed up; however, all of the pupils were there by the end of the week. That year Caroline and I were in the 5th Reader, and rode Pattie Bell to school.

Mr. Crow was kind to us all—and we all liked him. Most of the children got along and played well together, that is, except for a girl named Estella. She was real rough and seemed to always cause trouble.

One day she stole Sydney's pencil, then said she didn't have it. Caroline and I expected she did, so I got her to let me try on her belt. When I felt her waist I felt the pencil, so Sydney took her pencil which caused a minor row.

Another day Estella pulled Victor Huffman out of his seat. Then she boxed his ears, making him mad. So he picked up a stick and hit her, making her cry.

Otherwise, things were pretty normal until school was over the 1st of August. We were kind of sad to see school let out this early because we really enjoyed it. But Mr. Crow made it a happy day by giving all of us candy and raisins as we left for home.

Later that summer we discovered that Papa had arranged for us to attend school in Joseph that fall, so we were in for a new experience—leaving our one-room schoolhouse on the Divide, moving to town to live in a new house, and having Grandmother to look after us for the school term.

Memorable Times

Not too far from the cabin there was a lovely big rocky cliff on the south side of the hill where we could play in the early springtime and gather buttercups when the snow was still on the hilltop. This cliff we called Darling Castle, after one in a story. My name was Lady Lillian Darling—I wish I could remember Caroline's name. The cats and our dog Rover would go along and enjoy the sunshine and the fresh green grass to play in. We had a wonderful time, but, unfortunately, we always returned home with ticks on us.

During our ten years on the homestead there were lots of memorable times, some good and some not so good. . . . .

I remember that Christmas was always a grand time to look forward to, but that first year on our homestead Christmas had to be very plain as we had no money to spend on presents, or no way to get to town even if we had had the money.

Aunt Lou and Uncle Tommy in Missouri had sent a package for Grandma's family and us sometime before Christmas. I recall how disappointed we all were, as they were our only rich relations and we thought there would be something nice for everyone. But when the package was opened there was a whole bolt of the ugliest calico I have ever seen. It was dark brown with big circles of lighter brown, and white streaks here and there. Papa said it looked like *Thunder and Lightning*. There was also a bolt of dark brown cotton flannel. Mama said, "I will not make dresses for the children from that calico. It will make good comforters and quilt linings." The men in the family had to wear underwear made from the cotton flannel, and Steve said, "I'm ashamed to undress before the other men in the bunkhouse during harvest." It lasted and lasted. I remember Caroline and I made lots of little brown rag dolls from scraps of the cotton flannel when we played *Robinson Crusoe*, after Papa read the book to us.

Caroline and I had china dolls from the previous year; Caroline's doll's name was *Clara*, after Cousin John's new wife, and I called mine *Eva* for Eva Trimble, a neighbor's daughter whom I much admired. Mama sat up nights and sewed on new dresses and underwear for the dolls long after we were asleep. The new dresses were made from a pink lawn skirt that she had had in Missouri, and as the basque was worn out it had been laid aside until it could be of some use. The dolls' dresses each had a lace collar and a blue bead for a *breastpin*. The underwear was white muslin and was also lace-trimmed. Christmas morning the first thing we saw was our dolls sitting all dressed up on the mantel-shelf. And they did look beautiful. Then our stockings had, first, a big popcorn ball, then a huge lump of brown sugar, and, finally, a darning needle. We always thought a darning needle was something extra—why, I can't now imagine. Anyway, that was our bounty. We were thrilled and didn't feel that anything was lacking this wonderful first Christmas on the homestead.

Our Aunt Allie and Uncle Steve were great ones to play jokes and tease. Even Grandma was full of fun, but Mama was like our father—rather sedate and serious.

One day when Allie, Caroline, and I were at home alone, Allie got a little white turnip from the garden, cut thin curved strips, and made terrible long ugly teeth on one side of a strip. She put them in her mouth where she held them in place between her lips and gums. Then she tied a red bandana handkerchief over her head, wrapped Mama's big red shawl around her and suddenly appeared before Caroline and me. "I'm an Indian and I'm going to eat you up!" she said in a voice that sounded strange because of the turnip teeth in her mouth. Although we knew it was Allie it scared us nearly to death. Papa heard us screaming and ran from his work to see what it was all about. He had to laugh when he saw Allie, and was unable to scold her very convincingly.

Another time Allie, Caroline, and I were piecing quilts and tacking carpet rags. Allie, being older, had pieced two quilts. Caroline was working on her first, a *four-patch*. We were always so happy when someone gave us some pieces of cotton cloth for our quilts. Every scrap was used. Those too narrow to cut for quilts were kept for the rag rug we hoped to have someday. Mama said she would give us five cents a pound for all we tacked, so we were trying to see who could get the first pound. Steve was there and he could see that Caroline was far behind. He took off his suspenders, and turning his back to the rest of us, he wound Caroline's tacked rags around the rolled-up suspenders. She didn't say a word, and when Mama weighed our balls everyone was surprised that Caroline was ahead.

That evening when she said her *Now I lay me* prayer, she whispered to Mama and told her why she was ahead. "First I thought it was funny, and I wanted to win, but now that I have told you, I feel better."

Great-uncle Jeff was very special to my mother, and her voice was different when she spoke to him, as she loved and honored him. In return he was very fond of her family, but I knew from the first that he didn't care for me as he did for my sister or Allie. I was always to blame for things. Once, when he was taking care of us while Mama was away, Allie teased me till my temper got the better of me and I called her a skunk. Uncle heard me, and to punish me he put me under the big hen-coop out in the hot sun, and placed a rail on top so I couldn't get out. And so Mama found me, fast asleep with a dirty, tear-stained face.

Another time, in early spring, Uncle Jeff was staying at our house. He was fond of long walks. The snow was going off in places, and the loveliest of wildflowers, snowflowers as we called them, were blooming. They were white, with a tiny red center, and were very fragrant. Well, Uncle Jeff came in from his walk with a bunch of these flowers, the first sign of spring after six months of being shut in by snow, and he gave them all to Caroline!

I was crushed. Of course he couldn't have known how much I had wanted some of them—I am not through wanting some of them yet.

—◇◆◇—

A picnic was planned for the Fourth of July of 1890. Such marvelous food was being prepared by my mother—a big pan of fried chicken, the most wonderful fresh bread with buttered, golden-brown crusts, pickles, jelly—everything home-made, of course. Salads were almost unkown, though we had lots of little green onions and tender new radishes. But, Papa declared he would stay home and rest. "Why should I go and watch Steve and Tressie spoon all day?" he asked.

Steve came for us in his big three-seated wagon bright and early. We drove across Three Buck and up the awful hill to get Mrs. Shaw, Tressie and her sister Helen, who was just my age. Tressie sat on the front seat with Uncle Steve, and then Mrs. Shaw, Mama, and Caroline on the seat behind. Helen and I sat in the back of the wagon box on hay, with an old clean quilt to protect our Fourth of July dresses. We drove past our good neighbors, the Needhams, to pick up Welthy, her brother Will, and Will Shaw. Welthy, I recall, was quite put out that she hadn't had time to blacken the twine strings that she used as shoe laces.

The country was so young and our hearts were so gay as we drove over what felt like the worst road in the world. As we were going over the Cat's Back with our flags flying, we could look across Coyote Gulch and see our ranch, and there in the field of fresh young grain was Papa walking with Rover at his heels. This picture kept rising before Caroline's eyes and she would say, "I hope Papa and Rover are having a good time too."

We went down The Cat's Back, a long narrow ridge, for several miles, then down into Bear Gulch. The winter before must have been really severe here, for there were dead cattle on all sides. At last we came to a wide little valley of sorts with immense rocks, like castles, scattered about, and free of carcasses. We decided that this was a good place to eat and found a spot of shade. So the horses were tied to the back of the wagon, where they calmly proceeded to eat our hay seat, as we youngsters started out across the creek to explore before lunch time.

We found a little deserted shack, where, probably, some poor deluded homesteader had tried to make a living, then, as I thought, had starved out. We ventured inside the sad little house and there found a pile of old magazines. Oh, what a wonderful find! The magazines were water-stained and old, but we didn't mind. They were something to read, and had pictures of beautiful actresses in them. I was so excited over the magazines that I clean forgot to watch out for the sight of Tress and Steve spooning, as I had planned to do.

Mama and Mrs. Shaw spread out our dinner, and Oh what a dinner! A fairy stream babbled down the gulch and its delicate windings seemed strangely out of place amid the rugged surroundings. Was ever our glorious stars and stripes set up in such a place before?

We started back after a very enjoyable day. The ride home seemed rougher than when we started out, due somewhat to the fact that the horses had eaten our hay seat. But, despite the bumpy ride, we were thoroughly happy with our treasure of old magazines.

As the team pulled the wagon up on the last rise of the Cat's Back we could look across Coyote Canyon and see our homestead perched on that high grassy plain. We could hardly wait to get home and tell Papa all about our wonderful Fourth of July outing.

Uncle Jeff was a great organizer. He loved to go up into the timber and search for huckleberry patches, then go get a bunch of friends and relatives to go picking. So it was arranged to ask the Rumbles to go with us for an overnight berrying. Uncle Jeff was *Commander*. We had a pack horse, as we had to take blankets and food. I hated to leave Caroline, and wished that she, Grandma, and Papa could go with us, but I knew Papa was happy not to have to go. He never liked picnics, or things of that sort, and it wouldn't be too pleasant for Grandma or Caroline.

Uncle Jeff, being a good leader, took us right to the good berry patches. We staked our horses where they could get their fill of the tall grass. We didn't have a tent, but it was warm, so we spread our blankets over the fir boughs the men cut for our beds. Sitting around the campfire listening to Uncle Jeff and Mr. Rumble tell stories about Indians and wild animals was fun, but it got very dark all around us where the firelight didn't reach. Mama and Mrs. Rumble soon had a nice supper of potatoes baked in the hot ashes, fried ham, bread, butter, and jam. There was coffee for the Rumbles, and the rest of us drank fresh mountain water.

Soon after eating we all went to bed. Uncle Jeff, Mr. Rumble, and Steve on one side of the space, with Mrs. Rumble next to her husband. I was so tired that I went right to sleep, but was rudely awakened by what I thought was a coyote, but Steve said it was a timber wolf. He got up and heaped more logs on our fire and said, "I guess that ham smelled good to the wolf." So we all went back to sleep. The next thing I knew Mama and Allie were both gone, but I heard them talking as Mama led Allie back to bed. I realized that she had been sleepwalking and was, in fact, still asleep. Mama rummaged in her pocket, found a piece of twine which she tied around one of her toes, and the other end around Allie's toe. "Now I can sleep, knowing she can't get out of bed without my feeling the string pulling."

Mama said next morning that the wolf howling disturbed Allie. She got up and struck out through the timber in the direction from which the howl came, and all through the night she would start to get out of bed whenever she heard the howl.

Breakfast over, we decided to go home as we had all the berries we could take back, and all were tired, even I, though it had been lots of fun. When we got home Grandma said, "I think Caroline and I should go the next time you pick huckleberries."

So the next week just our family went, but not quite so far, so we could be back home by evening.

Grandma was a very excitable person. If she got a shoestring, apron or sunbonnet string tied in a hard knot, she would go into hysterics. She always said she *smothered*. Mama asked the doctor if it could cause any real harm to her, and he said indeed she could die from it. So the family watched out for her spells.

It was quite a task to get her on the horse, as she hadn't ridden for years, and we had no sidesaddle. They put a soft blanket over Papa's saddle and she mounted from a block. So we got started. Mama and Caroline on Coalie, Allie and I on one horse, and Steve, of course, on another with the bucket and our lunch.

The place we went, because there were no high hills, was thickly covered with very tall thin trees. There were some nice berries there, and after the horses were all unsaddled and staked out, we got busy picking. It was a hot day, and as the timber was so dense there wasn't much of a breeze. To see the sky one would have to look straight up, and there would be a little bit of blue.

We hardly got settled when suddenly we all heard Grandma making a fuss. Mama told Steve and Allie that Grandmother was smothering, and to get the horses quickly. "We got to get her out of here or she will die!"

We gathered everything and rushed Grandma home. This proved to be one outing that we never forgot. Needless to say Grandma never wanted to go again.

How the cattle country people did hate sheep! We children, heard it discussed so much that we would not have been surprised to see a sheepman with horns and a tail!

So, it was not surprising what we did one day on our way home from school. Caroline and I rode Old Coalie, and our friend, Helen Shaw, rode her very own horse, an old bay pony with a knocked-down hip. His name was Freighter because he had long ago been used in a freight team. We saw, to our horror, a big band of sheep slowly moving along near John Fine's fence, eating our cattle's grass all up. This wasn't the first time that sheep had trespassed on our property. I remember Papa riding out several times to warn the herder to keep the sheep off of our land. And once Pete Bedan ordered his man to herd the sheep across Three Buck Creek, all around the schoolhouse, and over on to the John Fine place. We felt we should do something about it at once so we could tell our folks and the children at school about it. Our plan was to ride as fast as our fiery steeds would go, right through the herd, and perhaps cause a stampede. So my sister took a firmer hold of my garments on each side as Helen and I changed from riding sideways, as was considered proper, to riding straddle, and away we went. We charged right through the gentle sheep—what confusion— clouds of dust and bleating of lambs lost from their mothers! We didn't feel so brave when the angry sheepherder confronted us with a gun. But when he saw what had caused the disturbance he laughed and told us to go home. We must have looked queer, as Freighter had a most peculiar gait, owing to the knocked-down hip, Caroline and I had on slat sunbonnets, and Helen, a boy's old felt hat. We didn't feel like bragging about our adventure after all, although we had been doing our bit toward ridding the cattle country of the enemy sheep.

That summer we had been bothered a lot by one of the big cattlemen's two-year-old steers. He was what my father called a *knot-head*, a little roan range animal that had never had any care other than being branded and having his ears marked. He had taken up with our cows, and was always right at the gate, ready to dart in with our cattle to get a lick of salt from the huge lump kept in the corral, or a gulp of water at the water trough. One evening is impressed upon my memory. It was very hot and dry. Three or four of the dry young stock were being let in at a time to get their allotment of two buckets of water each. Well, as usual, here was the Knot-head, looking through the planks of the gate and seeing the other cattle getting a drink. His little eyes were red and he bellowed hoarsely and tried to slip in with each bunch of cows. The water had to be drawn up from the well and poured into the hollowed-out log that served as a trough. My sister and I sat on the fence and watched, trying not to feel sorry for the Knot-head. At last, all our cattle had been watered and I saw our little, slim mother, her body leaning far over from the weight of a huge full bucket of the precious water. She opened the gate and, to our suprise and gratification, set the water down in front of the Knot-head. After all these years I can still feel the glow of pride and love that welled up in my heart for our little work-weary mother, who, from her meager store, could yet spare a cup of water even to an enemy.

My mother, to my childish eyes, was at that time strong, brave, and well able to care for us alone, but now as I look back I see her—a slim young thing, very timid and shy, with smooth, black hair and big hazel eyes.

The year that Grandma and Allie went back East, our neighbors, the Walter Bunnells, gave a party. They had built a new frame house, and as their daughter Lucy was having her eighteenth birthday, they decided it would be a good idea to celebrate by having an old-fashioned country dance.

The day before the event a man drove up in a one-horse buggy. It was really was a novelty in the West at that time to see a one-horse rig, roads being what they were. A single horse had to walk either in the center of the road, where it was rough and full of rocks, or to one side, which caused the vehicle to travel with two wheels off the road. Our visitor proved to be a minister, what they called a *circuit-rider*. He asked to spend the night, saying, "I would like to leave my buggy here, as I go as far as the Snake River, and there are only trails, no wagon roads. If you can use the buggy you are welcome to it."

Caroline and I were jubilant, for we thought right away how nice it would be to go to the dance in a buggy. Papa would drive, Caroline would sit on Mama's lap, and I could squeeze in somehow. We talked and planned all day. Mama told Papa we would do the chores early and eat a cold supper, for the Bunnells would have a big supper at about eleven o'clock. We wouldn't start home till daybreak, as the roads were too rough to drive over in the darkness.

Mama always boasted that she never saw the day when her children did not have a decent outfit, in case we wished to go someplace. We were to wear our best woolen dresses, and would black our shoes. Mama and Papa looked fine in the clothes they kept to wear to town. Papa admired his new shoes. He had very narrow feet and loved good shoes.

After a snack of bread, jam, and milk, Papa said, "I have the harness on Coalie. I'll hitch her up in the corral. You open the gate so I won't have to get out." It was a lovely mild fall day, and we were all happy, except Rover. Mama had said, "You will have to stay home, Rover," and he understood her and sat down looking sad.

All at once we heard Papa yelling and the buggy rattling. We hurried out, thinking he wanted the gate opened. But the buggy, with Coalie hitched to it, was backing instead of going forward. She was afraid of the buggy, and having it hitched to her was more than she could stand. Papa and Mama tried every way to get her to move forward, but it was no use. She just wouldn't.

"Well," said Papa, "We'll just have to stay home." Caroline and I began to cry. Mama said, "We intended to walk before we had the buggy, and the children are not going to be disappointed. We are going anyway." Papa said, "I am not walking like poor white trash. You and the children can go." So we took the harness off Coalie, put on a blanket, surcingle, and bridle, then we returned to the house where we heard Papa throw his new shoes on the floor!

Mama and I took turns riding. Caroline, of course, rode all the way. I think it was around four miles, but we enjoyed it all. We saw Mrs. Drumhill coming just as we got there, and she was walking all alone. Walter Bunnell took Coalie to the barn, and we went with Mrs. Drumhill into the house. I felt very shy with so many people I had never seen before. Caroline and I sat on the plank bench that extended all the way around the large room of the new house which was to be divided into several rooms when the party was over. The old log house, which I always liked better than this new frame house, had a big shed-kitchen where the long plank table was set up. Even this early in the evening it was loaded with food—baked ham, fried chicken, cakes, and pies. Before salad was common, at least in the West, cucumber pickles, pickled onions, and cole slaw took its place. Coffee and tea would be served with the supper. Also hot buttermilk biscuits, jam, and jelly. The ladies that didn't dance would assist Mrs. Bunnell with the supper. Mama was one of these; so, Caroline and I had an excuse to see what was going on in the kitchen as well as on the dance floor.

Lucy Bunnell looked like an angel, I thought. She was blond and slim, and kept her complexion and hands white and pretty. She came running to us when we entered the house, saying, "Where is Mr. Wasson?" Mama told her he wasn't coming and she nearly cried. "I wanted him to play *The Old Rose Waltz* for me on my birthday. Nobody can play it on the fiddle like Mr. Wasson!"

They had an organ, and several men from the area took turns playing the fiddle. They played mostly square dances along with a few waltzes. The Huffmans were there alone as they had left their children at home with the grandmother. They surely enjoyed dancing. Mr. Huffman even asked me to dance with him. I hung back and said, "Oh, I can't! I don't know how!" He got me on the floor into a square dance anyway. I knew we looked funny, he being over six feet tall and I four feet three inches, but we had fun and I didn't do too badly. Supper was served at eleven o'clock. Mr. Bunnell announced, "Choose a partner and march to the table." Right away someone pushed Ernest Brown, a school friend, to my side. We were shoved along together and had to sit by each other. Being the youngest couple there we got teased. For instance, Ernest was served his coffee in a mustache cup! But the supper was grand and it was the first time I had ever been to a late party. It was the custom to dance the first dance after supper with your supper-partner, but Ernest and I were so shy that we wouldn't even go into the other room together. There being two doors, he came in one and I the other. How the grown-ups all laughed!

Shortly after supper Mrs. Bunnell asked Mama if we were tired. "There are two beds upstairs," she said, "and you can lie crossways. The beds are wide, and at least you can rest." Caroline and I declared we were not sleepy but Mrs. Drumhill said, "I am very tired, and the four of us can rest on one bed." We took off only our shoes, and, to our surprise, one moment we were listening to the music, and the next thing we heard was Mama saying, "It's time to get up, children. We have a long walk home, and Papa will be looking for us." Lucy wrapped up a big piece of cake for Papa, "Though," she said, "he doesn't deserve it, after disappointing me about *The Old Rose Waltz*."

The party was over, but it would long be remembered as the first gathering of its kind to be held *between the Sheeps.*

Papa and Rover were waiting for us, and when I gave Papa the cake and told him what Lucy had said about the way he played waltzes, he looked sorry he had not gone with us. Mama said, "I will get dinner a little early for I am thinking you didn't cook much breakfast, and the girls and I have had a long walk. We will all be hungry." But when dinner was on the table I did not feel like eating the good sausage and baked potatoes, and Mama asked if I was sick. I meekly answered, "I ate a big doughnut, a piece of gooseberry pie, a piece of cake, and a lot of pickles for breakfast." The guests that had stayed overnight at the party were invited to help themselves from the remains of the food before going home the next morning, and I had done just that.

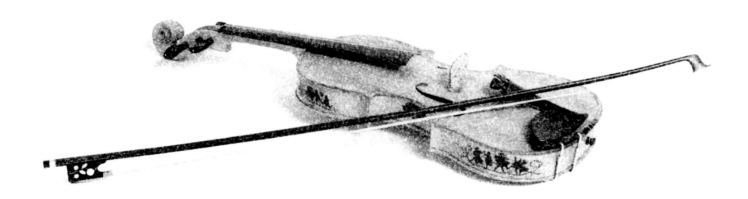

Not long before Papa's decision to move from the homestead, our kind neighbors, the Matt Prices, were in great trouble. Matt had been found guilty of cattle rustling between Idaho and Oregon and was in the Idaho Penitentiary. We heard that he had escaped and was being searched for. Papa was away from home, working in the valley at harvesting, and Steve was doing some fall plowing and skidding logs out to build a new home in the spring. We never thought of locking doors as a rule, but that night Mama said, "I'm locking up tonight. Who knows what can happen in times like these?" It sort of made me afraid and I didn't sleep well. I thought I was dreaming when I heard a tapping at the shed-kitchen door. I lay still and listened. The tapping came again, so I called, "Who is it?" and we heard Steve answer, "Jinks, it is Steve. Don't make a light, but let me in." So Mama opened the door, asking, "What is the matter?" Then he told her. "Matt Price is at my place, came in after dark. He was sick and hungry and had sore feet, so I fed him and gave him some clean rags to wrap his feet in. I let him have a blanket and he is sleeping in the barn on the hay. I waited until I knew he would be asleep, then ran over here in my sock feet, so he couldn't hear me. What shall I do, Jinks? He came to me for help, and I hate to give him up."

Mama didn't take long to ponder her answer. She said, "Steve, this is a new country, and if we don't obey the law none of us will be safe, or our property. You go for help. I believe John Rumble will be the best. He is older, and will know what to do. Be careful going past the Price place. There may be someone guarding them or even expecting Matt, and they might try to stop you."

I was all excited, and I don't believe Mama nor I slept any more that night. Along toward morning we heard a wagon pass on the way to Steve's place. We got up and dressed, and a short time after we saw Mrs. Rumble driving their spring wagon with Mr. Rumble and Steve in the back seat with Matt between them. He had his hands tied behind him, and looked so tired and sad that I wished he could escape. Steve told me afterwards that when Mr. Rumble and he told Matt to hold up his hands, he said, "I didn't think you would do this to me, Steve," And Steve replied, "I didn't like to do it, but you broke the law and have to pay." So Matt was turned over to the sheriff at Joseph and was returned to the penitentiary in Idaho.

There was a small reward for Matt's capture. It was divided between the Rumbles and Steve. Also, a gold watch was given to Mrs. Rumble for her part in the capture.

Mama's cousin Rat, always a wag, composed the following verse about the event:

There was a brave lady on Sheep
Who captured Matt Price while asleep.
With shotgun and chain
She forced him to remain,
And they gave her a gold watch for to keep!

We heard some time later that Matt had put soap suds in his mouth and acted wild, like he was insane, thus convincing the prison doctor who sent him to an asylum. Fortunately for him he wasn't there long before being released. About that time his family moved to Colorado and we all hoped that he joined them there and *lived happily ever after*.

Following the Matt Price event cattle-rustling became rare. So Steve and the Rumbles, with Mama's advice, had a share in establishing law and order in this part of the West.

I vividly recall the year the cellar collasped, when we lost a lot of our food. It was late in the fall and Mama said, "Children, we have had to spend most of our money for fruit and such things, to make up for our bad luck losing all our canned stuff. So we must not expect much for Christmas this year. We must just be thankful that we are all well, and have plenty of food to eat, and enough wood to keep us warm."

"Won't we have any Christmas at all?" Caroline and I asked.

"Yes," Mama answered. "We will have things we can make, and we will have a nice dinner. Steve will be here, and I think we will have a good Christmas."

As it turned out this Christmas proved to be one of our best, for Grandma sent us a package from Missouri—a Dutch doll apiece for Caroline and me. Papa named mine *Gretchen*, and Caroline's *Katerine*. Also included for each of us was an autograph album, something that we both had longed for.

Along with this was another surprise. A neighbor had brought up the mail a few days before Christmas, and with it was a big package from Papa's Aunt Kate in Colorado. I still remember how excited and happy we were when we saw what Aunt Kate sent. For Caroline, enough lovely blue cashmere for a dress, and for me, soft red woolen. Also, enough pink lawn for each of us a summer dress. And, wonders of wonders, a box of coconut candy that looked like strips of bacon. We made it last a long time.

I have always hoped I could find some candy like that again, but perhaps it wouldn't taste half as good.

Perhaps the most memorable Christmas of all was the next year. We had received some parcels late in the fall. The not-to-be-opened package was stored upstairs on one of the summer beds, and when I was sent up for sugar or other things it was a great temptation not to peek. One package was torn a bit, and, I'm sorry to say, I did tear it a little bit more. I could see some dark smooth wood, but that was all.

Just before Christmas Mama was making popcorn balls, taffy candy, and chocolate fudge. Also cookies cut in fancy shapes. Some were boys and girls with currant eyes. She had no cutters except a plain round one, but she did well with what she had.

Christmas morning, when Papa got the fire going well, and it was warm enough, Caroline and I scampered over the cold floor to the rag rug before the fire. There on the mantel were several packages. And our stockings held *store* candy, nuts, and chewing gum. Grandma had sent Caroline a beautiful China doll and a pretty wooden pencil box with the first colored pencils we had ever seen — red, blue, green, yellow — besides several good black pencils with erasers on them. And I have never received a present that gave me such joy, or that I loved as well, as the wonderful lap-writing desk of dark wood that awaited me. It was beautiful as well as useful as it had a place to keep stationery, letters, pens, pencils, and an ink bottle. There wasn't any ink though, as it would have frozen before I got it.

And that wasn't all. On Mama's trip to Joseph, Mr. Wurtzwiller had said to her, "There is a package for Daisy Wasson, left here by Lulu Coverdale. She said for me to keep it until someone from between the Sheeps came down."

When I opened the package I said, "Lu didn't forget, for here is my doll!" And such a doll! Bisque head and arms, eyes that closed, and real hair—all dressed in white, with ribbon bows! Mama put a strip of cloth under the arms and hung her from a big nail on the wall. There we could all see her without getting her dirty, and it was a good place, for when a neighbor came with children it saved worry, for they could just look and admire her without handling her.

I named my doll *Winifred Evangeline*. She gave me so much pleasure, even though I was going on twelve years.

Now, upon opening my trunk and viewing my prized possessions saved since I was a child on the Divide, I see my little writing desk. I feel a thrill something like when I first saw it that Christmas over sixty years ago. And after all that time I realize that I had Mrs. Huffman and her feather fan to thank for making my dear mother understand that no matter how practical the red flannel petticoats may be, it is the white feather fans that bring sheer joy and happiness to one's life.

Thinking back to when people would ask, "Why in the world did your folks ever come to this Godforsaken place when they could have stopped in the Grande Ronde Valley?", I have a picture in my mind of Caroline, standing, listening. She has on a little white linen hat, and is holding her walking sticks and leaning a little forward. I watch her, then after a bit, ask what she is doing. "I hear music," she answers, "when I am real still and look at the mountains, I hear it."

Little sister, life has held many disappointments, but if we hold still and listen we may yet hear the music.

Daisy Wasson

Historical Notes

After emigrating with his family to the Wallowa Valley of northeast Oregon in 1855, and finding all of the good land taken up, Joseph Wasson decided to homestead a plot of land on the Divide, a long open bench just south of the Cat's Back ridge which separates Big Sheep from Little Sheep Creek. There he constructed a new log home and settled his family in the summer of 1886. The cabin site was quite isolated, with the trip to Joseph being eighteen miles, and the closest neighbor over two miles away. During the Wasson family's ten year stay on the Divide a barn was constructed to shelter the stock, and a cellar and smokehouse were added to help the family become self-sufficient.

Daisy attended the first Divide School in 1887, with Caroline following a year or two later. As was quite common with children, the family pets became an integral part of their lives—as Caroline wrote in her diary of their most favorite: Topsy the colt was born in 1892.....their cat Croppie disappeared on the 5th of June in 1896, and when she failed to show up the children feared that she had been caught by coyotes—their father found her dead in the field five days later.....and Rover lived for about a year after the family left the homestead. And Hecate, good hen, lived to be twelve years old, a long life for a hen.

Joseph sold his cattle to a Mr. Neal on September 11th of 1896, and he and Jennie bought a house in Enterprise on the 15th. The girls left the homestead on October 4th to stay with their Aunt Allie in Enterprise while attending the Wallowa Academy. Their father rented a shop in Enterprise for $6.00 per month, and started a stationery-candy-tobacco business for which Jennie made bread, candy, cookies, and popcorn balls. The Wassons ran the business and lived in Enterprise for eight years before Joseph's ill health forced them to move away from the Wallowa Valley.

Their homestead on the Divide was sold and changed hands over the years, and is now owned by Bill Cool and his son Dan of Joseph. Of the original homestead buildings, only remnants of foundations remain to indicate the location of the original structures. However, to stand on that homestead site today, one can't help but be captivated by the awesome view—much the same as the Wasson family was so many years ago.

Joseph & Jennie Wasson

Joseph Wasson was born June 7, 1849 in St. Louis County, Missouri. His wife, Jennie Blevans, was born June 29, 1861. They were married in 1878 and had two daughters—Daisy and Caroline. Before the girls were old enough to attend school, the family emigrated to northeast Oregon where Joseph took up a homestead on the Divide ridge east of the town of Joseph. After ten years there the family moved to Enterprise so that the girls could continue their schooling. Joseph gave up the ranching life to be a small business operator, but his ill health forced a move to Vancouver, Washington in 1904. He and Jennie resided there the rest of their days, with Joseph passing away in 1923, and Jennie in 1944. Both now rest in the Enterprise Cemetery.

Daisy Wasson

Caroline Wasson

Daisy was born September 14, 1880 in Missouri. After emigrating to Oregon with her parents and sister, and living ten years on the family homestead, she attended the academy in Enterprise. A few years later she married Chester Turley, who worked for the Pacific Power and Light Company in Enterprise. Their first child was nationally known from the 1930s through the 1950s as Clare Turley Newberry, writer and illustrator of children's books. The Turleys moved from Wallowa County to live in Vancouver, Washington, where their second child, Joseph was born. He later became a design engineer with the Buick Motor Company. In 1953 Daisy and her husband moved to Flint, Michigan where they lived the rest of their lives, with Daisy passing away in 1969.

Caroline was born November 13, 1882 in Nevada, Missouri. At the age of twenty months she contracted spinal meningitis which left her impaired for the rest of her life. After leaving the Divide homestead in 1896 and finishing high school at the academy in Enterprise, she attended Whitman College in Walla Walla, Washington. While there she met, and later married in 1909, Calvin Cornelius Thomason. The two became writers and teachers, with Caroline authoring many articles which were published in newspapers and magazines. She also authored two books, one of which was *In the Wallowas*, an especially popular volume in northeast Oregon as it was a true-to-life depiction of Wallowa County history at the turn of the century. In 1910, the Thomasons had one daughter, named Corneil after her father. Corneil married Ray Hughes; they now reside in Joseph, Oregon. Caroline passed away in 1925, and she and her husband now rest in the Enterprise Cemetery.

Grandmother Blevans   *Steve & Tressie Blevans*

Grandmother Caroline Bartlett Hoskins Blevans was born in 1835 and married Robert Blevans in 1860 in Missouri where they raised six children, including Jennie Wasson, born in 1861; Stephen, born in 1868; and Allie, born in 1875. In 1885 Grandmother Blevans, with Stephen and Allie, emigrated to Oregon with the Wasson family. As soon as Steve was old enough he took up a place on the Divide just east of the Wasson homestead. His sister Allie lived there until her marriage to George Hyatt of Enterprise. Steve's mother also stayed with him until her death in 1899. It was there on his homestead that Steve built a new home before marrying his neighboring sweetheart, Teresa Shaw on March 28, 1892. The couple remained there until Tressie's death in 1925.

It is said that after his wife's death, Steve moved away from the homestead and tore down the house he so carefully built for her; however, he remained in Wallowa County where he was a popular life-long resident and served as a county commissioner for many years. He lived until 1946, and now rests with his wife in the Prairie Creek Cemetery east of Joseph. George Hyatt left his mark on Wallowa County with the E.M. & M. Co. building on the main street of Enterprise, and the elaborate Victorian home which he built, and a part of which still stands on the southeast corner of courthouse square. Allie lived there until 1925, preceding her husband in death by two years. They both now rest in the Enterprise Cemetery, as does Grandmother Blevans.

Daisy & Caroline Wasson
September 5, 1900

Illustrations.....

Illustrations (Cont.).....

The Bear Wallow Story

The Bear Wallow was formed in 1976 with a commitment to help preserve our Western Heritage through excellence in publication. From the beginning we have strived to carve a niche in the world of book publishing by developing a distinctive style of design—richly blending illustration with storyline, sparing little to offer one-of-a-kind limited printings suitable for any coffee table, library, or classroom. Our goal is to make history interesting and entertaining to readers of all ages while creating editions that are valuable to any collection.

Our first endeavor under the sign of the Bear Paw was in 1978 with the release of *Rendezvous*, a lavishly illustrated story collection of northeast Oregon history depicting the change in the country since the coming of the white man. In 1980 we released *Traces*, stories from the last still-living Oregon Trail pioneers who came West by covered wagon. We saw a great need to amass the early history of the Oregon Country—from discovery to settlement, so, *Where Rolls the Oregon* was developed in 1985 from diaries and other writings of sea voyagers, trappers, mountain men, and pioneers, with the storyline sensitively blended with photographic illustration to re-create the mood of the countryside in the early 1800s. In 1987 a letter that was brought to our attention became the catalyst for the creation of *A Letter Home* which depicted the early history of the Oregon Trail through the letter, diary exerpts, pioneer writings, photography, and artwork. In 1988 the epic history of the American West was captured with a fascinating collection of short stories combined with a wonderful collection of historic photographs in *An American Vignette*.

Around the Cat's Back is our most recent publication to combine artistic innovation with historic accuracy and fine printing to continue our commitment to book publishing as a work of art.

— Other Books by the Bear Wallow —

Rendezvous...ISBN 0-936376-00
Traces...ISBN 0-936376-02
Where Rolls the Oregon..............................ISBN 0-936376-03
A Letter Home...ISBN 0-936376-04
An American Vignette.................................ISBN 0-936376-05

Jerry Gildemeister
AUTHOR-DESIGNER-PHOTOGRAPHER

Although he had never traveled beyond the Mississippi, Jerry grew up with a fascination for the American West. His first taste of the real West came with summer work with the Forest Service in northern Idaho. From that time on he vowed to return, and did just that with his forestry career in 1955. However, his stay was rather brief, being interrupted by a two-year stint in the 82nd Airborne and the Special Services of the U.S. Army, after which he returned to resume his forestry positon in Union, Oregon. Concurrently, he seriously pursued a second career in photography, and eventually the photography won out. He now shares a home-based studio in the sagebrush foothills of the Wallowa Mountains with his wife Cathy and cat, Miss Poo.

In addition to their fine-art photography and Bear Wallow publishing, Jerry and Cathy offer a wide range of consultation, photography, design, and publishing services.

Jerry & Cathy Gildemeister

Don Gray

Don Gray
ARTIST

Exhibiting as a professional fine artist in museums and galleries across the United States, Don occasionally puts on his illustrator's cap for a new Bear Wallow publication.

A northeast Oregon native, Don had a very personal reason for his involvement with *Around the Cat's Back* — his ancestors are in the book. The Huffman Place that Daisy Wasson first visited was settled by John Huffman, Don's great-great-uncle. Doing research for the illustrations gave Don the opportunity to visit the Huffman homestead and other places so often mentioned by his folks and in his family lore.

Don lives with his wife Brenda near Union, Oregon. They have three children, Heather, Melissa, and Jared.

In Parting

I wish to thank all who have been involved in our projects. Though they are too numerous to list, they are not forgotten, as they have been the life-blood that has maintained the Bear Wallow commitment these past several years.

Furthermore, I am forever indebted to my wife, partner, and co-worker — Cathy, who has made these projects possible. Above all, I am especially grateful for the long hours she has endured in the darkroom to create the photo imagery for our books.

Only through such dedication and craftsmanship has it been possible to maintain the quality for this lasting tribute to our Western Heritage.

Jerry Gildemeister